C

D1394119

ALAN RACE

CHRISTIANS
AND
RELIGIOUS
PLURALISM

Patterns in the Christian Theology
of Religions

SCM PRESS LTD

290

0334 02555 9

First published 1983
by SCM Press Ltd
26–20 Tottenham Road, London N1
Second edition 1993

Printed in Great Britain by
Biddles Ltd, Guildford and King's Lynn

20023202

CONTENTS

Preface to the Second Edition   vii

1 The Problem   1

2 Exclusivism   10

3 Inclusivism   38

4 Pluralism   70

5 Incarnation and the Christian Theology
   of Religions   106

6 A Question of Truth   138

7 Ten Years Later: Surveying the Scene   149

   Notes   168

   Indices   181

For Christine

PREFACE TO THE SECOND EDITION

Slowly, both the church and the Christian theological faculties of the Academy are learning to see that interest in the encounters between the Christian faith and the world religions represents more than a passing fashion for those who happen to indulge in such matters. From a position of relative obscurity as part of 'any other business', the issues of those encounters have now become a prominent item on the total theological agenda. This can be illustrated by the simple fact alone that the number of publications dealing with the Christian theology of religions and inter faith dialogue has multiplied dramatically during the ten years since the first edition of this book.

There are material reasons why the encounter between the religions is assuming importance. They are to do, first, with the shrinking globe. The peoples and cultures of the world are 'thrown together': Africa and the Middle East are now in my living room; and mud huts in Indian villages have televisions. More locally: awareness of the multi-cultural and multi-faith texture of our towns and cities is becoming apparent at every level – in schools, neighbourhoods, prisons, hospitals, businesses and so on. A second reason why the encounter between the religions has assumed importance has to do with the knowledge that the globe is threatened. Historically, the religions have fostered deep hatred between peoples; or at the very least they have made little impact in overcoming such hatred. If they are to contribute differently, towards a brighter future, they must learn to cooperate. That, in turn, will entail the beginning not only of revised attitudes towards other religions, but also of change in the self-understanding of one's own. We survive or sink together.

There are also theological reasons why the encounter between the world religions is becoming significant. The religions claim that life is permeated by a reality that transcends what can be seen and handled. Yet the characterization of that transcendence is often very different in the different traditions; and sometimes utterly different. How then should Christians respond theologically to the experience of what I have come to call the 'transcendent vision of human transformation' ('salvation', to use the Christian term) at the heart of the religiously other? That is the task of the Christian theology of religions, which is now beginning in earnest.

From the perspective of Christian missions, the task is a troubling one. For if one purpose of Christian mission is to seek the inculturation of Christian faith, how should that proceed in relation to another culture which, historically and dominantly, has been informed by another religious vision? To respect other religious traditions as contexts of 'salvation' goes against the grain of the sense of unsurpassable finality or absoluteness, centred in the Christian belief about Jesus, that has motivated the Christian mission for centuries. But the task is also puzzling for the academic community, where it blurs the safe boundaries between the Religious Studies and the Christian Theology departments. For students of religious studies are challenged to take the *theological* dimension of the history of religions more seriously; and theologians of one faith-community are challenged to expand the range of *religious* data by which they come to a knowledge of the human relationship with ultimate reality.

The purpose of this book was both to develop a typology as a means of bringing some order to the range of positions being canvassed in the Christian response to the other world religions, and also to argue a case for a more pluralist approach as the way forward. While any piece of theological writing is bound to need further qualifications from the vantage point of ten years later, I nevertheless remain convinced about the value of the typology and the direction of the theology that I adopted then. The final chapter of this second edition of the book argues these points further, and in doing so assumes a working knowledge of its earlier sections.

Christian self-consciousness has undergone profound changes as a result of the encounter with critical thought, especially with the challenges posed by historical, scientific and philosophical studies. We can expect no less, once religious studies becomes the new dialogue partner. Many will wobble at the prospect. Others who have begun the journey tell of its enormous benefits. Who we are is a function of our interdependence.

1

THE PROBLEM

To say that we live in a religiously plural world is not new. What is new, however, is the increasing awareness that this brings with it serious theological issues for the Christian church. The days of religious and cultural isolationism are at an end. To the seeker the religions jostle with one another in a market-place of possibilities. Is the presence of God to be found only within one community of faith? Or is he more chameleon-like than that, dancing through history, enticing men and women into faith irrespective of the cultural shape of their response? And how does the Christian view the market-place of possibilities, realizing that the reason for his being a Christian at all is probably as much to do with his birthplace as it is with what he holds dear in his heart? These are major questions which strike at the core of Christian conviction.

Though the church has not been unfamiliar with religious pluralism in the past – Christianity itself came to birth in the Judaic and philosophical/mystery-religious milieu of the ancient world – the present experience transcends any earlier sense Christians may have had of its significance. In order to see why this is so, it is possible to specify at least three ways in which the new awareness is being borne in on the Christian mind. First, changing patterns of mobility have shattered older conceptions of the religious history of the world which viewed the faiths as confined, culturally and geographically, within particular boundaries. Personal contact between men and women from different cultures and faiths, at work or in a neighbourhood, is becoming increasingly commonplace. But with the technological revolutions in travel and communications the meaning of neighbourliness now has a global

I

application. The notion that the world is becoming a 'global village' implies personal contact between persons of different religious and cultural affiliations. Second, at an academic level, a wealth of knowledge has accumulated over the last two hundred years about the non-Christian faiths. The so-called 'history of religions' school, sometimes termed 'comparative religion', has amassed an enormous store of detail concerning the beliefs and practices of the world's faiths. In this light, ignorance about the world's religious history can only be regarded as culpable ignorance, a state of affairs which cannot be condoned when one comes to the theological problem of the relationship between the faiths. Finally, we can mention the new missionary consciousness which a number of ancient faiths are manifesting throughout the world. Due partly to the effect of the Christian missions, and partly to the political awakening of the ancient cultures to the cut and thrust of international relationships in the modern world, the ancient cultures (particularly in the Middle and Far East and Africa) are placing a renewed emphasis on their historical pedigree. It is not only Christianity or Islam, traditionally two of the most vigorously missionary-minded faiths, which consider mission to be an intrinsic part of their religious vocation; Hinduism and Buddhism, for example, are becoming almost as energetic in their missionary endeavours. For these three reasons, then, the fact of religious pluralism is being forced on the Christian mind as the context for its life and thought, and the church is summoned to make some sort of theological response to this most recent phase in its history.

The Christian theology of religions is the attempt, on the part of Christian theologians, to account theologically for the diversity of the world's religious quest and commitment, a diversity which shows all the signs of continuing to exist, in spite of the Christian missions. With Wilfred Cantwell Smith we may express the nature of the challenge before Christian theologians, posed by the new pluralism, thus:

> From now on any serious intellectual statement of the Christian faith must include, if it is to serve its purposes among men, some doctrine of other religions. We explain the fact of the Milky Way by the doctrine of creation, but how do you explain the fact that the Bhagavad Gita is there?[1]

The Christian theology of religions is the endeavour to adumbrate 'some doctrine of other religions', to evaluate the relationship between the Christian faith and the faith of the other religions. This is the urgent task before the church as the world'advances towards some form of unity implied in the term 'global village'.

The definition given here of the Christian theology of religions is very loose and has a limited working applicability unless it is qualified further. Before we do this, however, it is worth highlighting the paramount significance of the challenge to the Christian church represented by the new awareness of religious pluralism with reference to the remarks of two Protestant theologians, Max Warren and Paul Tillich. In an address given in 1958, Canon Max Warren, then General Secretary of the Church Missionary Society, said that the confrontation between Christian belief and agnostic science will turn out to be more like child's play when it is compared to the present challenge to the church in the encounter between Christianity and the other world faiths.[2] This remark is all the more pertinent when we remember that it stems from a distinguished Christian leader who was deeply involved in the missionary work of the church, and who came eventually to see that the old-style confrontation between Christianity and the other faiths was no longer appropriate. It was arrogant and theologically naive to assume that only Christians apprehended religious truth. His attitude was summed up in some words which have since become famous:

> Our first task in approaching another people, another culture, another religion, is to take off our shoes, for the place we are approaching is holy. Else we may find ourselves treading on men's dreams. More serious still, we may forget that God was here before our arrival.[3]

Warren was not one to foreclose the possibility that the disciples of non-Christian ways may be wrong or misguided. But that conclusion could only be the fruit of humility: Christians first taking off their shoes and endeavouring to listen attentively and as unprejudicially as possible to another's religious convictions. His main point, however, stands: out of the real encounter with men and women of non-Christian faiths the Christian is forced back to reconsider his understanding of those faiths; and this is likely to pose an even greater challenge to Christianity than the clash with agnostic science.

The second remark comes from a lecture Paul Tillich gave towards the end of his life. The future of theology, Tillich said, lies in the 'interpenetration of systematic theological study and religious historical studies'.[4] Tillich's own theological contribution was primarily directed towards answering questions raised against Christian conviction by science and philosophy, as these had developed over the last two centuries. But after two years of seminars and meetings with Mircea Eliade, one of the world's outstanding authorities in comparative religion, he discovered that Christian theology must travel another route if it is to survive. His own experience was that in contact with the history of religions 'every individual doctrinal statement or ritual expression of Christianity receives a new intensity of meaning'.[5]

If Tillich is correct in his judgment, then the future of the Christian theological enterprise is indeed at stake in the attitude the Christian adopts to the newly experienced religious pluralism. It is this linking of Christian systematic theology with the history of religions in a positive engagement, as necessary for the future revitalizing and self-understanding of Christianity itself, that Tillich draws to our attention when we speak of the significance of the awareness of religious pluralism as the milieu for Christian faith and practice.

The gradual focussing of attention on the encounter between religions as the new religiously and theologically important fact of our time has not remained, however, solely the concern of interested theologians. In the last twenty years the issues raised by this encounter have become the concern also of the institutional churches. Following the Second Vatican Council, the Roman Catholic Church established a special department in the Vatican, the business of which was to seek co-operation in dialogue with non-Christian faiths. In 1979 the World Council of Churches published *Guidelines on Dialogue with People of Living Faiths and Ideologies*, which was the fruit of ten years serious dialogue across religious boundaries. The *Guidelines* were commended to the members of the World Council for study and use, and in 1980 the first British commentary on the proposals was published by Kenneth Cracknell entitled *Why Dialogue?*, accompanied by a commendation from the British Council of Churches. Both reports recognize that dialogue between the faiths takes place on a number of levels, ranging from the day-to-day encounter between individuals pursuing their ordinary work in the world to the meetings between those who act as spokesmen for 'official' faiths or ideologies. Underlying all these encounters is the persistent problem of the criteria by which the Christian is to evaluate the relationship of his own faith to that of his non-Christian neighbour. In other words, he is challenged to formulate a Christian theology of religions.

I turn now to qualify further our initial definition of such a theology. Two aspects of it amplify its meaning. First, the matter is viewed from within a Christian framework. The other faiths will have their own approach to the problem – that is, where they have become conscious of it. It is a task which confronts the theologian of Christian faith, and not, say, the historian of religion or the student of comparative religion. As many have come to realize, it is not possible for the theologian to place his own faith in parenthesis while he examines the faith of others. Some expositions of the Christian theology of religions have come dangerously close to this at times, and they require to be corrected. What the Christian theologian must do is strive to listen attentively to the faith of the non-Christian as this is unfolded by the believer himself, without pre-judging that faith and without abandoning his own commitment as he proceeds. He is then ready to evaluate his own faith in the light of what he has heard, and evaluate the faith of his neighbour in the light of his new understanding of the ways of God's revealing and saving work throughout history. This is the twofold process of the Christian theology of religions suggested by J. A. Veitch. Yet it is this attitude of not pre-judging the faith of the other partner in the dialogue that is most problematic, and therefore most vital if the whole exercise is to succeed. Veitch's own working definition is most liable to this pre-judging tendency when he specifies it as

> the theological interpretation and evaluation of the claims made by believers in religious traditions other than Christianity.[6]

In my own definition I have purposely built in more flexibility than Veitch by focussing on the *relationship* between the faiths, viewed from within the Christian faith, rather than the straightforward evaluation of one set of claims by another, Christian set of claims. This leads to the second qualification of the definition.

The recognition that religions are not petrifications, but live continuously in process, adapting and changing in the light of new circumstances and new knowledge, is relatively recent. But it is important to grasp, for the implications involved if it is taken seriously are far-reaching. Without it, the tension between holding on to one's own confession and maintaining an openness to other religious commitments would be intolerable. The dynamic quality of religious faith and practice can be demonstrated in the Christian case by reference to the encounter between Christianity and the insights deriving from the modern disciplines of science, linguistic philosophy, and history. These disciplines have posed serious intellectual and theological problems for Christian faith, which has had to adapt itself as a result to assure its own survival. Effects of the clashes between these intellectual pursuits and Christian theology are still being experienced today, and have become a dominant part of the forum within which Christian faith is challenged to give an account of itself. There is no reason to expect that the effects of the encounter between Christianity and the other faiths will be any less profound. Yet it may be that the adaptations which Christian theology has had to make as a result of the rise of the new forms of knowledge will turn out to be of great assistance in helping Christian faith face the next step. A reified faith is much less likely to be open to other forms of faith than one which has learnt adaptation in the field of serious intellectual debate. A less reified conception of one's own Christian faith, and a less dogmatic approach to what is possible to be affirmed, are good preparations for a sensitive and honest Christian theological response to the fact of religious pluralism.

Alongside the growing awareness of pluralism as a theological problem there has been a substantial increase in the literature dealing with the subject. Needless to say, as the subject is still in its infancy there is no consensus among theologians about the outcome. But there is a need to co-ordinate the diverse opinion now emerging under the umbrella heading of a Christian theology of religions. This is not to say that attempts have not been made in the past to classify the very different approaches to our subject. One of the watersheds in this regard in Britain was the work of

The Problem

Owen C. Thomas in his *Attitudes Toward Other Religions* (SCM Press, London 1969), which classified the Christian response to religious pluralism under the headings: Rationalism, Romanticism, Relativism, Exclusivism, Dialectic, Reconception, Tolerance, Dialogue, Catholicism, Presence. Thomas's method was to gather together the writings of individual theologians, each of whom were introduced with a brief commentary outlining the general position of the writer concerned. His achievement was thus to indicate the broad sweep of the approaches to our subject. Other works which describe general trends in this field are Carl F. Hallencreutz's *New Approaches to Men of Other Faiths* (WCC, Geneva 1970), and Eric J. Sharpe's *Faith Meets Faith* (SCM Press, London 1977). These two writers were concerned to plot the historical and theoretical pattern, mainly in the present century, of the changing nature of the Christian theorizing about the other faiths. In this study I adopt the headings Exclusivism, Inclusivism and Pluralism as a broad typological framework within which most of the current Christian theologies of religions can be placed. The method I espouse is both historical and analytical, though mainly the latter, and proceeds by selecting individual writers as representatives of a particular theological position. Each heading contains within it a number of different options or variations on a theoretical type, and the differences between these variations are largely a matter of emphasis on the part of the particular writers concerned. The general theoretical type indicated by each heading remains the constant factor which warrants the inclusion of a number of approaches under the one heading. Finally, in any discussion of the relationship between Christianity and the other faiths, the place of the doctrine of the Incarnation must be accorded special treatment, for it is this doctrine which is generally thought to be the distinctive mark of Christianity and the touchstone of its 'doctrine of other religions'. We shall consider the place of the Incarnation in the Christian theology of religions from two perspectives: as a problem in Christian theological debate in the light of recent philosophical, theological, historical critiques; and the form it takes in the various theologies of religions themselves. A concluding chapter picks up the theme of truth in religion and considers the problems of the conflicting truth-claims of the world faiths. This is, of course, a theme running through all the chapters, but it

7

receives more detailed treatment at the end. Though the main intention of this study is to classify and arrange its material in a typological pattern, thereby concentrating on major selected theologians for the purpose, it is impossible for me to conceal my own predilections in the process. This will be obvious as the reader delves into the text proper. At any rate it cannot be avoided in a study of this kind, so it is as well to mention it at the outset. In the final chapter I take the liberty of pointing out the direction which I see the Christian theology of religions taking.

In one sense the Christian concern to formulate an appropriate theological response to the other world faiths is not new. The church has not been unaware of other world faiths at different periods in its history. I have already mentioned the intensely religious environment into which Christianity was born. Then in the seventh century Christians were confronted by another missionary religion in the form of Islam; and finally in the sixteenth century Christian friar missionaries experienced a real meeting with the Asian faiths. It is against this inherited history that the church seeks to formulate a theological response to the fact of religious pluralism as the new context for Christian life and belief. Whilst it is impossible to ignore the shape of the Christian response to the other faiths in these early encounters, I must also stress that they should not be allowed wholly to determine the Christian response now. For there are new factors in the current debate. The novelty concerns the unprecedented rise in the so-called historical consciousness, bringing with it the seemingly intractable problem of what is often termed 'relativism'; the extensive knowledge of the world faiths now at any scholar's disposal; and the general thrust towards dialogue as the appropriate mode of relationship between religious communities. Given these new factors, it is more imperative than ever that the church formulate a Christian theological response to the other world faiths. It may be that the dialogue between faiths which has only recently begun will alter the whole way in which the problem is now perceived, and we will discover that the concepts and categories we now employ to tackle the question will be transcended. If that is the case, we must be open to the possibility that any Christian theology of religions which is formulated today will turn out tomorrow to have been merely provisional. This possibility should not, however, deter us from

8

the responsibility of seeking a Christian theology of religions in the present. To that task we now turn.

2

EXCLUSIVISM

Not even the most detached reader of the New Testament can fail
to gain the impression that the overall picture of Christian faith
which it presents is intended to be absolute or final. It is indicated
in general themes and by specific texts. With regard to the latter,
the ones which most readily spring to mind are the words of Peter
in Acts 4.12: 'And there is salvation in no one else, for there is no
other name under heaven given among men by which we must be
saved,' and the words attributed to Jesus in the Fourth Gospel in
John 14.6: 'I am the way, and the truth, and the life; no one comes
to the Father, but by me.' The negative evaluation of other faiths
which these two texts suggest is hard to ignore. Furthermore, what
the New Testament indicates, the church has, on the whole,
endorsed through the ages. Undoubtedly, the predominant attitude of the church through Christian history has been to regard
the outsider as in error or darkness, beyond the realms of truth
and light. More than simply an expression of popular piety, it was
institutionalized and enshrined, for instance, in the axiom of the
Catholic Church, *'Extra Ecclesiam nulla salus'* (Outside the Church
no salvation), which has, until recently, played a decisive role in
the Roman Catholic Church's relations with adherents of other
faiths. Pope Boniface VIII is often cited as one who has stated the
axiom in its strongest exclusivist sense:

> We are required by faith to believe and hold that there is one
> holy, catholic and apostolic Church; we firmly believe it and
> unreservedly profess it; outside it there is neither salvation nor
> remission of sins . . .[1]

Exclusivism, however, has not been confined to the pronouncements of the Catholic Church. The same note was dominant in the three great Protestant International Missionary Conferences at Edinburgh (1910), Jerusalem (1928), and Tambaram (1938). It also formed the predominant attitude of the World Council of Churches, at least up to 1966, the year which ended the General Secretaryship of Dr W. A. Visser't Hooft. A new departure was inaugurated when the Central Committee, at their meeting in Addis Ababa in 1971, first adopted an 'interim' policy statement and guidelines on dialogue with members of other living faiths and ideologies. But this current stress on dialogue places a strain on the kind of relentless exclusivism which the churches have upheld in the past. For it carries within it a potential threat to the traditional belief in the uniqueness of Christ and Christianity. Those who defend exclusivism in the Christian theology of religions generally do so in terms which seek to expose that potential threat. They would all be likely to agree with the words of Hendrik Kraemer:

> What is truth in religion? is more urgent and more obscure than ever. This question is particularly urgent for Christianity, because it claims as its source and basis a divine revelation which at the same time is claimed to be the standard of reference for all truth and all religion.[2]

Exclusivism can be viewed as the exegesis of this citation from Kraemer. It counts the revelation in Jesus Christ as the sole criterion by which all religions, including Christianity, can be understood and evaluated. The inspiration for the exclusivist theories comes chiefly from the Protestant theologians Barth, Brunner and Kramer. We shall consider these writers in turn, bringing out the differences of emphasis between them, and then raise some questions concerning their method and interpretation. In a later section we shall cite the recent work of Lesslie Newbigin, who has attempted to answer some of the criticism levelled against the earlier expositions of exclusivism.

The most extreme form of the exclusivist theory has been stated by Karl Barth in his *Church Dogmatics*, Vol. 1/2 (T. & T. Clark, Edinburgh 1956), under the heading, 'The Revelation of God as the Abolition of Religion'. Fundamental for Barth is the one guiding principle to which every theological concern is subject: the revelation of God in Jesus Christ, attested in Holy Scripture. From this standpoint the practice of 'religion' is dubbed unbelief, and 'the religions' are in error and sinful blindness. If we are to understand Barth correctly here, we need to see how these assertions are a direct implicate of his understanding of revelation. That is to say, revelation is a revealing about both God and man, and the judgment on 'religion' and 'religions' derives from both elements. In the first instance, as the self-manifestation of God, revelation declares something which is wholly new about God, a knowledge which could not come to man by any route other than by God's revealing it to him. This means that the moment the new knowledge is received by man as truth it simultaneously condemns every attempt by him, out of his human potentiality alone, to know God. Religion which is the attempt to know God apart from revelation is therefore an activity of unbelief:

> The genuine believer will not say that he came to faith from faith, but – from unbelief, even though the attitude and activity with which he met revelation, and still meets it, is religion. For in faith, man's religion as such is shown by revelation to be resistance to it.[3]

In the second place, revelation is understood as the self-offering of God on man's behalf to provide the means of reconciliation with him. This in turn means that when a man acknowledges the act of grace accomplished for his salvation, he simultaneously declares that he is unable to help himself, and cannot reach God apart from God's own gracious activity. Religion which is the attempt by man to justify or redeem himself apart from revelation is therefore an activity of unbelief:

> Where we want what is wanted in religion, i.e., justification and sanctification as our own work, we do not find ourselves . . . on the direct way to God, who can then bring us to our goal at some higher stage on the way . . . God in His revelation will not allow man to try to come to terms with life, to justify and sanctify himself.[4]

Barth's relentless determination is to defend the absolute free sovereignty of God to act. Both the reality and the possibility of

God's revelation belong exclusively with the divine initiative. Any attempt on the part of man to anticipate, predict, or supply criteria out of his own reason by which the gospel may be interpreted, is a direct contradiction of the meaning and act of revelation. Both the revelation and its reception in the consciousness of man, are the result of divine graciousness: 'Revelation is God's sovereign action upon man or it is not revelation.'[5] Here we see how Barth's views are grounded in his epistemology, and arise directly out of it. It leads, with utter logical necessity, to the radical separation between 'revelation' and 'religion', the feature which contains within it the justification for the judgment which this theory pronounces on the other faiths. The Christian gospel belongs with 'revelation', and the other faiths are the product of 'religion'. This radical separation, it is necessary to stress, is not the result of an exercise in comparative religion, but arises out of Barth's understanding of the Christian revelation. Furthermore, it explains why much of Christianity, when it is not centred upon the revelation in Jesus Christ, is condemned as are the other faiths. It is not Christianity as a developed historical religion, with its own structures and complex organization, which judges other faiths, but solely the gospel of Jesus Christ. Indeed, there is a sense in which Christianity, more than any other developed faith, stands condemned if it fails to obey the faith with which it has been entrusted. The church, as an institution, has no theological justification to view itself as superior to the other faiths. Nevertheless, Barth is anxious to distinguish 'right and true religion' from the variety of religious activity in the world, and in this he recognizes that the Christian stands more disposed to a correct orientation:

> At the end of the road we have to tread there is, of course, the promise to those who accept God's judgment, who let themselves be led beyond their unbelief. There is faith in this promise, and, in this faith, the presence and reality of the grace of God, which, of course, differentiates our religion, the Christian, from all others as the true religion.[6]

It follows from this that Christianity alone has received authority to be a missionary religion, and it has a duty to summon men and women from the world of the religions to follow the Christian gospel.

It is easy to misunderstand Barth's judgment on the world of the religions. Some have seen in it the most harmful and distorting bigotry, the product of narrow-mindedness and cultural isolation. This would certainly be to misrepresent his genuine theological concern, which is the defence of the absolute sovereignty of God. It is not out of a perverted Christian arrogance that Barth asserts the supremacy of the Christian way, but from sheer obedience, as he sees it, to the truth as it has been given in Jesus Christ. In fact Barth was quite willing to see the greatness of human achievement, art and culture that is reflected in the non-Christian faiths. He was not above praising what was beautiful and good in religion: 'In the sphere of reverence before God, there must always be a place for reverence for human greatness.'[7] Yet what Barth seems to have had is a keen awareness of the propensity for sin and idolatry that lies close to the heart of religious practices, and he has ample evidence from the history of religions to justify his sensitivity. This awareness would account in part for the extreme form of his so-called dialectical theology in respect of a Christian theology of religions. But a greater part of his extremism, and this includes now the polemical nature of his pronouncements, probably lies in his reaction to the liberal theology of his teachers. These tended to view Christianity as one form of religion alongside others, and its relevance in the world was measured against categories other than those of the gospel itself. For Barth, this led to error; moreover, it was an act of rebellion by man against the sovereignty of God. Therefore Christianity had to be proclaimed as *sui generis*, disavowing any collaboration with schemes which elevated a nominal notion from the history of religions to be the criterion which judged the Christian religion.

It is hard not to feel offence at Barth's theory because he states it in such extreme terms. Consequently, many of his disciples have pointed to his later writing as a better and more profound expression of his thought, claiming that it is possible to detect a change of mind there. In his *Church Dogmatics*, Vol. 4/3 (T. & T. Clark, Edinburgh 1962), Barth outlines the relationship of the Christian community to the world, and therefore also to the world religions. Is there, then, anything here which gives evidence of a change in Barth's approach to the other world faiths?

Essentially the Christian attitude to the world, and therefore to people of other faiths, derives, according to Barth, from the correct understanding of the Christian vocation, which itself is viewed in the context of the divine activity of grace. In the past the Christian claim to absoluteness often led to an arrogant missionary stance which saw evangelism as cajolery. The command of Christ in the Great Commission text at the end of Matthew's Gospel to *make* disciples of the nations for Christ was seldom interpreted other than literally. Barth rejects this as the least important answer to the Christian vocation. Christian truth is not a possession, but is to be witnessed to: 'The essence of their vocation is that God makes them His witnesses.'[8] As the locus of true religion (only as and when it lives by grace, of course) the task of the church is to declare to all people that Jesus Christ has died and been raised for them, that they already stand in the light of life:

> In each and every man to whom it is directed it is concerned, not with an actual, but certainly with a virtual or potential Christian, with a *christianus designatus*, with a *christianus in spe*. It is concerned with a creature ordained to know and realise his membership of the body of Christ.[9]

There is a new emphasis in this passage. As a dialectical theologian Barth insisted that God's Word, spoken to man in Jesus Christ, was always a paradoxical address consisting of 'yes' and 'no' simultaneously. The 'yes' referred to the new life which has already been won for him as a result of the salvation wrought by Christ, and the 'no' referred to man as he exists in ignorance of, or hostility towards, the gospel. The shift in Barth's thought is towards a greater emphasis on God's 'yes' and away from the polemical approach of his former period. Man must never be seen in terms of God's 'no', but always from the standpoint of the gospel as the creature who has a future in the body of Christ. In this Barth makes use of a distinction in the definition of man: as the subject of his own existence he is culturally determined both by his environment and his past, and as his own unique self is 'immediate to God and his neighbour' (Barth's phrase, p. 804). The person who is addressed by the gospel is approached by virtue of his 'immediacy to God' and only secondarily because he is outside the body of Christ. Although the question of the relation of the Christian church to the other faiths is never raised explicitly in this section of Barth's *Church Dogmatics*, it is obvious from these few brief remarks that the change in Barth's views is one of emphasis and not in his underlying theology of religions as it was presented in his earlier writing. A similar observation has been made by J. A. Veitch, thus:

> In volume one the *negative* side of the dialectic (between Revelation and Religion) emerges as a dominant factor and in volume four the *positive* side emerges to redress the balance.[10]

This means that the later work of Barth is continuous with his earlier essential conviction that 'We must not ascribe to him (i.e. man) any existence except as the possession of Christ.'[11] In the theology of religions this leads to exclusivism. The revelation of God in Jesus Christ reveals all humanity to be in need of the understanding, solidarity, and help of the Christian community, whether or not they acknowledge the fact. Men and women of other faiths are no exception to this.

There is something disturbing in Barth's unyielding approach to non-Christian faith. Is it realistic to pronounce on other faiths without a thorough prior knowledge of their beliefs and practices? It has been reported that D. T. Niles, a Christian theologian from India, in conversation with Barth, once asked him how he knew that Hinduism was unbelief when he had never met any Hindus himself. Barth's reply was, '*A priori*'![12] In the light of this kind of response one cannot help but sympathize with one commentator on Barth's views that his thesis that religion is unbelief is 'a product of the ivory tower', and 'the antithesis between religion and revelation is fictitious'.[13] However, we must remember that in the context of Barth's particular Christian assumptions his reply to D. T. Niles was entirely consistent. The effect is to see this way of stating the exclusivist theory and the general Christian theological assumptions behind it as possessing a 'take it or leave it' quality. We shall return to this effect of Barth's views later when we consider some criticism of other versions of exclusivism. In the present context it is appropriate to note further that even some who share Barth's general Christian theological stance have expressed doubt in knowing how to interpret satisfactorily his theoretical admonition of the other world faiths. Hendrik Kraemer, for example, who himself shared Barth's concern to proclaim the absolute sovereignty of God as the only possible method in Christian theology, thought Barth's over-emphasis dangerous and unjustified. Echoing what has already been said, Kraemer writes:

> However, there is something in the way in which Barth elaborates this with untiring energy and versatility that strikes one as artificial, somehow unreal, convulsive and overdone ... One does not feel that this is dialectical theology![14]

As Barth is hailed as the founder of dialectical theology, this last comment is something of an indictment of his application of the dialectical method in the Christian theology of religions. The real question, according to Kraemer, was whether the dialectical method could enlighten the proper *interpretation* of the religious life of mankind. In other words, do the non-Christian faiths reflect anything of the presence and power of God in any sense at all, and does any kind of divine initiative lie behind the world's manifold religious activity?

Kraemer himself sought to answer this question by the application of the dialectical method, as he understood it, more fairly to the biblical account of God's relationship to mankind. In spite of his former agreement with Barth, this meant that Kraemer's approach was more akin to the theology of Emil Brunner, a fellow-countryman of Barth's and the name most closely associated, after Barth's, with the dialectical theology they all espoused. Brunner's own words make it clearer what it means to be dialectical in relation to other faiths:

> From the standpoint of Jesus Christ, the non-Christian religions seem like stammering words from some half-forgotten saying: none of them is without a breath of the Holy, and yet none of them is the Holy. None of them is without its impressive truth, and yet none of them is the truth; for their Truth is Jesus Christ.[15]

In the same manner Kraemer recognizes the New Testament's witness to the presence and activity of God outside the revelation in Christ, and yet also its distorted apprehension:

> God works in man and shines through nature. The religious and moral life of man is man's achievement, but also God's wrestling

17

with him; it manifests a receptivity to God, but at the same time an inexcusable disobedience and blindness to God.[16]

The two aspects of the dialectical approach envisaged by Brunner and Kraemer are clarified in these two passages. First, there is the universal revelation of God to mankind through the moral law within and the created order without, and this corresponds to God's 'yes' to the world. Second, there is the perverted and distorted awareness of that revelation through sin and blindness. Both of these aspects of the explanation of the religious life of the world are revealed by the revelation in Jesus Christ. The breath of the Holy does indeed blow through the religions, so that God cannot be said to be absent from them, and it would be undialectical to dub them 'unbelief' *simpliciter*; but the new order which is established by Christ reveals also the distorted awareness that characterizes their heart, and which cannot be properly known without the light of Christ. In line with Barth, this form of the theory also distinguishes between the empirical phenomenon of Christian history and the ideal Christian gospel. Much of what passes for Christian history is also subject to the same kind of analysis: in the light of the ideal gospel Christian history is not immune from exemplifying the truth of the dialectical explanation of religious activity.

Two further comments can be added to this general sketch. First, Brunner and Kraemer are united with Barth in maintaining the distinction between 'revelation' and 'religion'. Recognition of God's revelation outside Jesus Christ does not mean that Christianity (again, when it lives solely by grace) is one species among others of the genus 'religion'. Both are agreed that there is no concept which can be said to arise from the phenomenological study of religion and be normative for understanding Christianity's relationship to the other faiths. Even outstanding representatives of theories which attempt to construct a Christian theology of religions on this basis are judged to have failed in their understanding of the real nature of the biblical revelation. Kant, who founded religion on the moral law within; Hegel, who related man's spirit to the Absolute Spirit; Schleiermacher, who justified religion as the feeling of absolute dependence; Otto, who interpreted religion as the experience of the numinous, grasped elements of the truth but not the complete truth. Ultimately these 'immanental' theories are said to fail to account for the sense of revelation, that in religion which has to do with powers which confront man from outside of himself. As Brunner expressed it:

> Apart from real revelation the phenomenon of religion cannot be understood.[17]

The dialectical account of mankind's religious history includes these theories, but with the introduction of the concept of revelation, goes beyond them.

In the second place, this dialectical approach does not involve Kraemer or Brunner in the concepts of 'natural theology' or 'general revelation' as they have been used in the Catholic tradition of theological enquiry. 'Natural theology' has functioned in Christian discourse in two senses: in a narrow understanding to provide a philosophical justification for the existence of God, and in a broader application to supply an epistemological framework or setting in which questions of revelation can receive meaning and truth. Both these uses imply, for these theologians, an impeachment of the sovereignty of God and are to be rejected on this ground. Kraemer's meaning of 'general revelation' when it is applied to the other faiths is not intended as a reference to the possibility of the authentic and saving knowledge and fellowship with God outside the Christian faith. It is a pointer to the dialectical nature of God's presence and activity in the natural world, conscience and culture, as it has been defined as a result of the revelation in Christ. This, according to Kraemer, is the true biblical perspective. All other modes of God's presence are to be judged from the gospel as it has been given:

> Since the Word 'became flesh' (incarnation) and equally because this same 'Word' is the eternal Logos, through whom all things are made and in whom is the light and life of man, it is impossible for Christian thinking to interpret God's revelation in nature, history and conscience as independent fields. Their interpretation can only be legitimately expressed in the light of the revelation in Christ.[18]

Kraemer takes both Barth and Brunner to task for failing to understand a proper biblical orientation over the terms 'natural theology' and 'general revelation'. In their famous controversy Barth and Brunner were not sufficiently idalectic, Kraemer said, in their handling of the biblical material.[19] Barth was too concerned to defend the traditional Protestant revolt against the use of such concepts in Catholic Christianity, and although Brunner came closer to a true understanding than Barth, he often lapsed into an application of the terms reminiscent of their traditional use.

Distinguishing modes of revelation does not lead to relativism in the theology of religions. It serves the more essential function of clarifying the christological perspective from which an exclusivist theory can be constructed. Kraemer makes his dependence on the doctrine of the Incarnation clear in the above passage. Brunner identifies the relation of Christianity to other faiths best in a christological statement:

> Jesus Christ is both the Fulfillment of all religion and the Judgement on all religion. As the Fulfiller, He is the Truth which these religions seek in vain. There is no phenomenon in the history of religion that does not point toward Him . . .
>
> He is also the Judgement on all religion. Viewed in this light, all religious systems appear untrue, unbelieving and indeed godless.[20]

Brunner's concern is to do justice to the elements of truth as they appear in the non-Christian religions and balance them against the Christian claim that 'Incarnation is revelation radically understood'.[21] Barth would have concurred with Brunner's stand on the centrality of the Incarnation in the Christian theology of religions, though he probably would not have expressed Christ as the 'Fulfillment' and 'Judgement' of the religions, except perhaps in his later thought. Kraemer, on the other hand, cited Brunner's words with approval.

We have seen how Kraemer's dissatisfaction with Barth led him to side with Brunner, who, according to Kraemer, was more dialectical in his approach. But if Kraemer was not a slave to Barth's thought, he was also not uncritical in relation to Brunner. This criticism highlights a further difference between these formative theologians of the exclusivist theory. It centres upon the extent to which actual knowledge of the other faiths is allowed a place in the final form of the argument. Barth, we have noted, formulated his position without applying any knowledge whatsoever from other faiths. Brunner advanced one step further and formulated his theory in the light of both the liberal accounts of religion and the claim to revelation as it appears in the other semitic prophetic religions. In this second respect only Judaism, Islam and Zoroastrianism (or Mazdaism, as Brunner called it) can claim to be a rival to Christianity. Religions of mysticism cannot make a claim to revelation, they can only point to it. Yet on closer examination even these prophetic religions are not free, believed Brunner, from self-assertiveness and self-redemption at their heart. Consequently they cannot be said to claim to be based on revelation in a comparable way to the Christian claim:

> The closer consideration of the facts of the history of religion therefore shows that the common assumption that the Christian claim to revelation is opposed by a variety of similar claims of equal value is wholly untenable.[22]

The Christian claim to revelation is accordingly absolute revelation. Kraemer praised Brunner for examining Christianity's claim to rest on unique revelation against the background of the other prophetic religions, but he lamented the limited use Brunner made of real knowledge of the other faiths. As a result his position still remained somewhat detached and he was therefore unable to give a thoroughly convincing answer to the problem of Christianity's relation to the other faiths. Kraemer moved a further step ahead of Brunner in a bid to rectify the apparent 'artificial' tone of Barth's original thesis. His achievement was to combine in one all-embracing theory Christian theological principles, based on what he termed 'biblical realism', and a detailed knowledge of the essential religious dynamics of the major non-Christian faiths. The result was a powerful justification of the exclusivist theory in the Christian theology of religions. As an indication of the impression Kraemer's work created, it is interesting to note that his book which carried the thesis, *The Christian Message in a Non-Christian World*, written for the World Missionary Conference at Tambaram in the same year as its publication, 1938, was praised by William Temple, who was then Archbishop of York, as likely to 'supply the principles of missionary policy for our generation'.[23] Historically Kraemer's work was immensely influential. The general outlook was shared, for example, by Dr W. A. Visser't Hooft, General Secretary of the World Council of Churches until 1966, and consequently that great international ecumenical body refrained from dialogue with the other faiths until after the end of his term of office. It is therefore important to examine in further detail Kraemer's basic arguments.

First, the 'biblical realism' which Kraemer sought to apply derived from the fundamental tenets of Christian neo-orthodoxy which was in the ascendant at the time. It followed Barth in asserting the absolute supremacy of God's revelation in Christ, but made some adjustments, as we have seen, in the area of biblical interpretation, to bring out more clearly the dialectical nature of the revelation it contained. The 'realism' did not refer to a stance on infallibility, but indicated the Bible's profound grasp of the essential religious realities, namely, the ultimate sovereignty of God and the sinfulness of man.

Second, Kraemer's study of the non-Christian faiths led him to view them as all-inclusive systems, each characterized by particular apprehensions of the totality of existence. Each system was an attempt to understand and interpret the existential condition of man, according to the different patterns which describe the basic core of the religions. This knowledge enabled Kraemer to compare the apprehension of the totality of existence as Christianity perceived it with the interpretations proffered in the non-Christian religions. The result was, of course, an exercise not so much in comparison as in contrast, corresponding to the distinction Barth had made earlier between 'revelation' and 'religion'. With Kraemer, however, the distinction had been given some empirical grounding in his actual knowledge of the non-Christian faiths. 'Discontinuity' became a key word to describe this position.

The combination of Christian theological principles and detailed study of other faiths, as they could be grasped from a phenomenological perspective, meant that in this first phase the other faiths were described by Kraemer as human achievements. This was at variance with his modification of Barth, which applied a dialectical analysis to the other faiths. Although he was critical of the traditional understanding of the terms 'natural theology' and 'general revelation', he did not wish to limit the divine initiative in other modes of revelation. So much he read out of the biblical account which saw God at work in nature and history as well as in Christ. In his later work, *Religion and the Christian Faith,* Kraemer sought to correct the over-emphasis in viewing the other faiths as human achievements and concentrated on the religious consciousness of man as the locus of God's activity outside the Christian dispensation. This kind of analysis was also present in his earlier writing, but now it received more penetrating treatment. Man's religious consciousness was truly a place of God's revealing presence, but at the same time it manifested a distorted response. There was, however, a serious consequence of Kraemer's renewed emphasis on man's religious consciousness. By locating it on the opposite pole to God's revelatory presence, it had the effect of reinforcing his earlier position on 'discontinuity'. This increased critical trend was expressed more forcefully in his final work, *Why Christianity of All Religions?*:

> If we are ever to know what true and divinely willed religion is, we can do this only through God's revelation in Jesus Christ and through nothing else.[24]

When this is applied to the other faiths Kraemer concludes:

> In this light and in regard to their deepest, most essential purport they are all in error.[25]

There is more than an echo of the early Barth in these words of Kraemer. This is not surprising in view of the fact that Kraemer's earlier correlation of Christian exclusivist principles with the phenomenological analysis of the non-Christian faiths was not pursued in his later work. Also, his post-colonial concern for inter-religious fellowship led him to stress the renewed humanity which Christ has made available for the world as an essential part of God's revelation as the Christian received it. This had the effect of emphasizing again the discontinuity between Christian faith and the other faiths. As can be seen, there is a parallel interest in Kraemer's stress on renewed humanity in Christ with Barth's later emphasis on God's 'yes' to the world given in Christ. The irony is that in Kraemer this coincided with a marked increase in maintaining the distinction between 'revelation' and 'religion'. Furthermore, it reinforced the obligation for missionary work among the adherents of other faiths. As Kraemer expressed this aspect of his theology:

> Surrendering to Jesus Christ means in effect making a break with one's own past, religiously speaking, however impressive that past may be and often is; and the Christian Church is in duty bound to require this break, because one must *openly* confess Him.[26]

The *raison d'être* for mission may be articulated in the language of revelation and necessary *witness* to it by Christians, but it nevertheless leads ultimately to seeking the conversation of individuals from non-Christian to Christian faith.

As it has developed, the exclusivist theology of religions has come to represent the most clear-cut of all the theories in this field. It involves no complicated theory about the nature of religious experience; it appeals to what for many is a self-evident biblical witness; it gives a central function to the person of Christ; the internal logic of the argument appears consistent and coherent; and, finally, it is the position which corresponds most closely to what has generally been held to be orthodox Christianity through the centuries. The question remains for our consideration: is the exclusivist theory an appropriate response to the new knowledge we now have about the world religions? In the way in which it has been formulated by these prominent theologians it appears impregnable. Is it possible for a more critical analysis to penetrate this apparent impregnability? There are a number of critical remarks which can be made about this approach in the Christian theology of religions, and most of them concern the attempts of Christian theology to come to terms with philosophical and historical studies as these have developed in the West, particularly since the Enlightenment. We shall consider a number of difficulties which philosophical and historical enquiry creates for this theory of exclusivism.

First, let us reflect on the sense in which the theory is logically impregnable. We noted above how Barth's thesis had an air of unreality about it. How much was this abated by Kraemer's inclusion of a phenomenological study of the non-Christian faiths? One wonders whether Kraemer, as he developed, had really integrated such a study into his overall theory when by the end of his life he reverted to a greater dependence on his purely Christian theological principles. Ultimately, it is possible to claim, the exclusivist theory functions independently of the knowledge of other faiths. In point of fact it is the product of a particular view of the notion of revelation. If Christianity rests on true revelation, it argues, then by logical inference the other faiths of mankind must be false or illusory. The empirical facts are irrelevant to the argument. But is it permissible in theological argument to deal with the mystery of God and man's relationship to him in so hasty a manner? Wilfred Cantwell Smith has made an interesting comment on this application from logical inference:

> It is far too sweeping to condemn the greater majority of mankind to lives of utter meaninglessness and perhaps to Hell, simply on the basis of what seems to some individuals the force of logic.[27]

Not all the tradition, however, has been so hasty in applying the kind of logic inherent in the exclusivist theory. For example, the Roman Catholic Church has not always applied the axiom 'Outside the Church no salvation' in the rigorist sense. Hans Küng has made the important observation that 'whenever this axiom in its *negative* formulation has been taken in the absolutely literal sense of the words it has led to heresy'.[28] This could, in one sense, be interpreted as a refusal by one major section of the church to be content with the rigorist approach. Pope Pius IX was the first to state positively and officially that ignorance of the gospel does not place a person outside the divine gifts of grace:

> The gifts of heavenly grace will assuredly not be denied to those who sincerely want and pray for refreshment by the divine light.[29]

By implication this is a refusal to theorize about the non-Christian faith according to the rules of strict logic.

Most versions of exclusivism show a kind of tacit agreement with the Catholic Church's judgment at this point. Even Brunner and Kraemer's dialectical approach admitted that there is light in non-Christian faiths. More recent versions of the exclusivist theory are emphatic that God's presence and activity is not limited to those who openly respond to it in the Christian sense. Lesslie Newbigin, for example, decries the attitude of those Christians who 'imagine that loyalty to Jesus requires them to belittle the manifest presence of the light in the lives of men and women who do not acknowledge him . . .'[30] But he goes a stage further than this when he says that the Christian theology of religions requires Christians to be prepared to learn from other faiths and ideologies as they encounter each other in dialogue:

> The whole Church itself is only learning, and it has to learn through open and humble dialogue with men and women who do not acknowledge him.[31]

Christians know only in part and must never give the impression that they have a monopoly of religious truth. Essential to Christian discipleship, believes Newbigin, is dialogue with other faiths and ideologies, the goal of which is to gain a greater understanding of the person of Jesus.

It is difficult to know how to evaluate Newbigin's suggestion that the Christian can learn about whom Jesus is from those who do not share a commitment to him, particularly in the context of exclusivism. Newbigin himself has also said that the role of the Christian in dialogue 'can only be obedient witness to Jesus Christ'.[32] Is there a contradiction here between 'learning' and 'witness'? Could it be that Newbigin is straining to maintain a hold on exclusivism which, for the purposes of realistic dialogue, ought to be surrendered? His intention, however, is stated more clearly when he cites the story of the encounter between Peter and Cornelius in Acts (ch. 10) as an example of the mutual learning process he envisages. In this story the church learns further about Jesus when a stranger to the gospel is converted and in the conversion brings a new understanding from his own background and cultural heritage to bear on his understanding of the person of Jesus. Translated to the present day, it implies that learning is not the result of the Christian listening to the Hindu, say, reflecting as a Hindu on the person of Jesus, but is a consequence of the Hindu offering his understanding of Jesus after his conversion to him. If this is what Newbigin means by mutual learning, then there is no contradiction with his exclusivism. But if he wishes to say more than this, then it is not clear how to assess his stance on exclusivism. Yet what is clear is that, in the period following Barth, Brunner and Kraemer, when dialogue is in the ascendant, exclusivism is developing away from a simple black-and-white picture which the theory suggests. If we are to be critical of the exclusivist theory now, we must penetrate more deeply the concept of revelation as it is applied by its protagonists.

All the exclusivist theories we have considered see the declaration of the absoluteness of Christ (and therefore, potentially, the church) as an integral part of the concern to defend the total supremacy of the sovereign freedom of God to act as he wishes. Barth, in particular, is so committed to this defence that even some of his devoted followers have criticized the air of unreality which surrounds his thought. It is the consequence of the heavy emphasis he places on the divine transcendence. Both the giving and the reception of divine grace is an act of God's graciousness towards man. The problem with Barth and the whole approach which he initiated is how to judge his emphatic stance on revelation. We can state the difficulty in a simple way: how does Barth *know* all this? There is a sense in which the stress on transcendence leads to a form of gnosis, so that only those who have been given the key to the door which unlocks the secrets of Christian knowledge can be saved. Though this is how it has appeared to many commentators, it would be a gross misunderstanding of Barth's concern. He can be defended against this kind of attack. David Ford, for example, has said why Barth refuses to allow any kind of criteria or reasoning derived from areas of knowledge, other than the strict concern to defend the sovereignty of God, to apply in theological discourse:

> Barth sees any such formal criteria, which are inevitably based on the norms of other areas of knowledge, as an infringement of the freedom of God to speak for himself, and a presumption that in the face of God one can step aside for a while to assess the situation neutrally. His confidence is that theology's object shines for itself.[33]

The strong commitment to divine transcendence (a position which is still maintained in Barth's later writing, despite his emphasis on the 'humanity of God' and the 'yes' of God to man in Christ) and the refusal to allow any kind of philosophical argument to determine theological method have led many to dismiss Barth in a few sentences, especially in Anglo-Saxon circles which tend to endorse an empiricist approach in theology. This dismissal is undoubtedly wrong when it is so premature. For Barth's theology is remarkable in its combination of coherence, rigour and conviction. Nevertheless, there is the recurring question: has Barth so isolated theological language that it is impossible to know whether or not what he believes is credible at all? Cannot man in some of his experiences and aspirations approach God outside the miracle of grace? Is theological knowledge so different from other forms of knowledge that it surpasses other forms of reason? One major source of hesitation in commentators' minds about Barth's account centres on the relationship that he draws between the event of revelation and the apprehension of it in the mind of the believer. God is said to be involved in both acts of the process and this is, presumably, part of the reason why we can have confidence that 'theology's object shines for itself'. Yet the intractable problem remains: if God does shine for himself, as Barth's epistemological model entails, then it involves the most extraordinary by-passing of the normal means by which knowledge comes before the human subject. Surely the medium through which we receive God's light is so much part of our ordinary world that we cannot help but judge and evaluate it from our position within the world. It is not that we cannot step aside from the light of God as it shines, but that we are unable to step aside from the world as we receive the light. If this is granted, then no matter to what extent we commend the belief that faith is wholly 'unmediated', such a belief will always seem an arbitrary judgment. No wonder many have seen an either/or decision here between Barth and his critics.

Those who remain unconvinced by Barth's method, because of the insurmountable epistemological problems as they see them, at the heart of it, will also view exclusivism as the least appropriate response to the relationship between Christianity and the other faiths. They will refuse to accept the validity of the distinction between 'revelation' and 'religion', and they will be open to the possibility that the knowledge of God outside the Christian tradition is not so qualitatively different from that of the Christian tradition itself. For as soon as one allows the normal means of human enquiry and reasoning a role in theological formulation, then one is open to the finite and the historical. It then becomes imperative for the theologian to account for the place of Christianity in the light of the total religious history of the world. He will need to account in his theory for the recognition that religions have originated and flourished in relatively isolated cultures and environments for most of their history. He will need to reckon with the fact that religion and culture are so inextricably linked that religious truth is always 'conditioned' knowledge. As Ernst Troeltsch expressed it, every culture is held together as a totality, *eine Totalität*. Given these kinds of assumption about historically conditioned knowledge, no faith which proclaims itself as absolutely *a priori* the true way can escape the charge of religious arrogance and imperialism.

The new historical knowledge of the other faiths gives rise to the possible theory that the religious traditions of the world are the result of an interaction between the divine initiative and the differing cultural and philosophical settings in which man lives across the globe. Inherent in this suggestion is the danger of relativism, the view which holds that all faiths are equally true, and therefore also equally false. An openness of this kind does not necessarily lead to the position known as relativism, and we shall discuss this aspect of the Christian theology of religions in a later chapter. That the tendency is in this direction is impossible to ignore, and many exclusivists consider such a view inevitable if one lets go of the emphasis on the sovereignty of God's revelation in Christ and the confidence that God's light shines and convinces according to its own luminescence. This is probably one of the strongest motives for retaining the exclusivist theory among those who adhere firmly to it. But strength of motive is one thing, credibility of the underlying theory is another. It is possible to interpret exclusivism as compromising the sovereign freedom of God, rather than as an infringement of it. To believe that the divine has been made known in different ways in different cultures according to different philosophical and interpretative forms does not, we may argue, undermine the sovereignty of God but enhances it. In this respect Barth was too hasty in reacting to the liberal theology of his teachers. Though Barth himself would not admit to it, he can be validly interpreted as perpetrating two theses in his exclusivism. First, the absolute sovereign freedom of God to act as he pleases; second, the belief that God has chosen to reveal himself exclusively in Christ. If the distinction here is valid, then we can value the first thesis and admire Barth's unrelenting concern not to compromise the freedom of God, whilst detaching ourselves from the exclusivity of the Christian way as a necessary implicate of the freedom of God to act as he pleases. We assent to A. K. Cragg's judgment of Barth s exclusivism, that it represents 'the dogmatic form of an overwhelming experience of grace and is to be appreciated, indeed saluted and celebrated, as such'. In which case, as he goes on to say, 'we can take its positive assurance without its negative privacy'.[34]

If Barth's position conceals an unresolved obscurity at its heart, how far can we say that his followers, who modified his extremism, provide an acceptable alternative? It may be thought that Kraemer's stance on 'biblical realism', with its dependence on personalities and lived history, offers an approach less redolent of the ivory tower. Is this the case? Kraemer himself expressed his dependence on the Bible thus:

> The Bible in its direct, intense realism presents no theology. It presents the witness of prophets and apostles.[35]

Presumably the implication of this witness is that the Christian way is the only ultimate way of truth, and all other religious ways are to be confronted with the self-evident reality that God has acted here in an unprecedented manner for the salvation of the world. Yet there are problems with this strong reliance on the Bible, in this particular form, and they are analogous to the philosophical epistemological problems present in Barth's approach. Just as we believe that it is impossible for theology to avoid some sort of reckoning with philosophy and the processes of the human mind in the apprehension of revelation, so it is impossible to avoid theology's reckoning with the results of historical enquiry into the biblical witness. Historical studies have made us so aware of the nature of the biblical material and how it has come to us that Kraemer's reliance on the Bible, in his particular form, now seems over-simple and naive. In the first place historical criticism has made us aware of the very real theological nature of the Bible. Witness cannot be divorced from theology, as Kraemer purports. The theological nature of the New Testament, for example, is manifested in the plurality of theologies it presents. Particularly with regard to the place of Jesus, we are now aware of the different responses to, and interpretations of him made by different writers. Different interpretations of Jesus are integrated with whole theological outlooks, circumstances and needs, in a way which questions the view that the writers are simply witnesses without theological bias and colouring. In the second place, historical enquiry has highlighted the conditioned character of the biblical knowledge. When Kraemer says that the Bible presents no theology, he shows no acknowledgment of the conditioned nature of the biblical accounts. For theological reflection belongs within a context and a cultural setting. It is bound up with cultural assumptions which are not always easily appreciated by people of other cultures. In the search for a Christian theology of religions this has the effect of making the Christian claim to absoluteness in the exclusivist sense appear arbitrary. Moreover, it is not necessary to go to the extremes of cultural relativism before one recognizes that there is a problem here for a faith which believes itself to be unique and universal.

We shall consider shortly the reaction of one writer who defends exlusivism against these implications of historical studies in theology. At this stage, we can note a preliminary effect of historical enquiry into the Bible, and into the New Testament in particular. It is this: the radical distinction between the gospel and the church, between Christianity as it lives by grace and Christianity as an empirical phenomenon in history, is unrealistic in view of our new knowledge of the nature of the biblical material. The New Testament is the product of the church and cannot be wrenched from its setting in the church without seriously distorting its import. It may be commendable to want to distinguish the gospel from the church, but the radical separation envisaged by the exclusivists is impossible to maintain as a result of the searching critique of historical enquiry. Furthermore, this impossibility is demonstrated by Kraemer when he attempts to specify the 'non-derivative, the primary "given" of Christianity', which is held to be the criterion which judges both 'the religions' and 'Christianity as a historical reality'. Formally this criterion is 'the Person of Jesus Christ',[36] and in more qualified senses it is 'Jesus Christ and His Kingdom',[37] or, 'Jesus Christ Himself and the quality of love revealed in Him'.[38] The alternatives proposed by Kraemer signify his dilemma. If the rather formal criterion 'the Person of Jesus Christ' is applied, then it is difficult to know how this would act in any satisfactory way, as the term is void of practical content. In other words, it is only when the term is given content that it can function as the criterion it is meant to be. But if the term is given content, as in the qualified uses we have cited, then an element of doctrine has been introduced into the criterion. This is to say, as soon as one moves beyond the formal definition of the criterion, one is involved in the critical reflections and doctrinal debates of the church as an empirical historical reality, which is therefore historically accountable. The radical separation between the ideal gospel and the empirical history of the church is unreal, because the person of Christ is mediated through a tradition of scriptures, sacraments and culture, and is not known apart from such mediation. Kraemer's criterion which judges the world faiths is as much derived from the doctrinal definitions of the evangelical tradition of Christianity as from a self-authenticating revelation which is said to be immune from historical criticism.

Exclusivism in the theology of religions is, generally speaking, more the product of Protestant than of Catholic theological circles. This is evident in the strong reliance on the New Testament as the starting-point for faith and the foundation for the Christian theological enterprise as a whole. However, the subjection of the New Testament to searching historical enquiry over the last two hundred years has resulted, for many, in the abandonment of the simple Reformation principle which operates in Protestant theology, namely, that the New Testament contains everything needful for faith. The strangeness of the New Testament world, highlighted by the new historical perspective, has led many to develop some kind of hermeneutical principle or tool to enable the New Testament faith to have application and challenge in the modern world. Yet the historical-critical method bites even deeper than the response suggested by the development of hermeneutical principles. For it has come to challenge, according to some scholars, the interpretation of Jesus as the unique Incarnation of God – one, if not *the* foundation doctrine of the exclusivist theory. If this challenge to the doctrine of the Incarnation can be sustained, Christian belief in Jesus as the final or sole channel for the revelation of God is less tenable, and the criterion that 'through Jesus

Christ alone' must the world faiths be judged rests on doubtful assumptions.

The issue of the Incarnation is discussed in a later chapter and the outcome of the current debate over that doctrine is obviously crucial to the exclusivist theory. For if it can be demonstrated that Jesus was God Incarnate, then it seems reasonable to suppose that the faith which sprang from his inspiration is the one which God intends men and women to follow, because it represents the declaration of God that this religious way is ultimately the only true way. If it cannot be demonstrated, however, then exclusivism would represent an unsubstantiated theory. There are of course a number of theological and philosophical, as well as historical, issues involved in the current debate surrounding the Incarnation. But we shall consider here some of the historical aspects, as these illustrate more readily the response by the proponents of exclusivism, since Barth and Kraemer, to the role of the critical-historical method in Christian theology generally, and its relevance in the search for a Christian theology of religions.

In general terms, the argument of those who apply the historical-critical method rigorously to the New Testament is that it may reveal the interpretation of the figure of Jesus as the unique Incarnation of God as a belief which was appropriate to the early centuries of Christianity but not necessarily binding in the modern world. The method would involve investigating the evidence of the New Testament without assuming the later doctrine, attempting to lay bare the motivations of the authors and cultural conditions within which the interpretation of Jesus took place. It would see Jesus first of all as a man of the first century who preached and acted in certain ways which evoked a profound response so that many became his followers. It would then attempt to uncover the links between the experience of Jesus' impact and the interpretations of his person recorded in the New Testament. Most of all, the method would see the doctrine of Incarnation as an interpretation which belongs properly as the conclusion of such investigations, whereas uncritical Christian theology tends simply to assume it. As a method which claims impartiality in the search for truth, the critical-historical approach therefore has much to commend it. However, the exclusivist response to the historical investigations of scripture, when these point to a denial of the doctrine of the Incarnation as the appropriate form of belief in Jesus today, is a refusal to accept the basic principle that the New Testament can be investigated in so impartial a manner. As Lesslie Newbigin has put it :

> One's judgment about the reliability of the apostolic testimony to Jesus will depend upon whether or not one shares their belief in the unique and decisive character of his person and work, or whether one seeks to interpret Jesus by means of models drawn from other experience.[39]

In other words, all historical investigations involve their own presuppositions which, in this instance, rule out the idea of a unique divine intervention in the person of Jesus as an integral part of the methodological procedure. According to Newbigin this is not a clash between 'faith' and 'history', but a clash between two methods of approach in the interpretation of scripture. One is the assumption that the event of Jesus Christ represents a unique intervention in history from beyond history; the other is the assumption that Jesus can properly be understood from within the Enlightenment view of history, which is the view that history is the unfolding of immanental forces in a continuous and unbroken relationship of cause and effect. The first assumption leads to the belief that Jesus is the centre of world history and that all history, including therefore non-Christian religious history, must be understood in relation to his uniqueness; the second assumption leads to the view which forfeits Jesus' role as the key to world history. Newbigin makes his case forcefully, and it is crucial to his exclusivist theory generally. What can be said by way of critical response to his challenge?

First, it is possible to say that Newbigin has overstated his argument by assuming the extreme dichotomy between two approaches to scipture. It is not the case that the interpretation of Jesus as a unique and final intervention in history by God himself is ruled out by the method and presuppositions of the modern historical method. Certainly an appeal to history would involve reservations about unique interventions until such a point in the study when it could be said to be necessary and inescapable as part of the total understanding of the events. Historical investigation, at any rate, could never *prove* the necessity or otherwise of the

Incarnation as an appropriate interpretation of the event of Jesus Christ. That always remains an act of faith anyway. What historical study could do is prepare some groundwork which may, or may not, point in the direction of the Incarnation as the only reasonable and complete interpretation of the life and work of Jesus. If Christian understanding is going to appeal to history in some way for its credibility, then it is hard to avoid this kind of procedure in relation to its sources and history. Newbigin does want to view the Incarnation as a judgment of historical evidence and inter-pretation, but only in a limited sense. The exercise of critical reflection is confined to the presupposition of Christ's uniqueness and is subordinate to it. If we ask how it is that he knows that the event of Jesus Christ represents God's unique intervention, the answer must be *sola fide*. At this point his position becomes logically invulnerable, and is analogous to the invulnerability of Barth's view of revelation. It is more the case that Newbigin has ruled out the possibility that Jesus can be interpreted in ways other than the Incarnation than that the Incarnation is excluded from the begin-ning by those who apply historical methods rigorously.

Second, the extreme dichotomy which Newbigin assumes be-tween two approaches to scripture leads him into problems concern-ing the supposed continuity or discontinuity in the relationship between Christian faith and the other faiths. In order to demon-strate the radical discontinuity between the gospel and the non-Christian faiths he posits the event of the cross as the key to true Christian understanding. As he has expressed it:

> In the light of the highest of human standards of truth and righteousness, Jesus appears as a subverter, as he did to the spiritual heirs of Moses, and as he does for the noblest and most sensitive among the adherents of other faiths and ideologies.[40]

Newbigin's point seems to be that at the level of highest commit-ment the non-Christian faiths prove themselves to be enemies of the Christian gospel. The cross is a scandal to the Jew and the Greek in the New Testament, but there is no reason, he believes, why this should not extend to all the non-Christian faiths. Again, Newbigin makes his claim forcefully, and the Christian is certainly obliged to place the cross at the centre of his faith. Yet how legiti-mate is Newbigin's conclusion? The stress he makes on discon-

35

tinuity is always at the expense of a stress on continuity. As far as
the latter is concerned, Newbigin sees this as possible only from
the side of the converted Christian. The trouble with this is that
it represents only one interpretation of the New Testament evidence. Continuity is as much a feature of the scriptures as discontinuity. As we shall see in the next chapter, continuity is a
recognizable feature of Luke's theology, and discontinuity more a
feature of Pauline theology. Furthermore, there is still a query
whether Newbigin's stress on the scandal of the cross applies in a
simple manner to the Eastern faiths, as he sees it applying to the
relationship between Christianity and Judaism. Christians might
find it necessary to hold on to the cross as the focal point of their
own faith, and as central for mankind's understanding of the ways
of God in his world, but it does not follow that adherents of other
faiths have no saving knowledge of God, or are enemies of the
gospel.

Wrestling with the place of revelation, the Bible, and the person
of Jesus Christ in Christian theology is the task of the Christian
theologian. Yet the process of articulation and formulation of
Christian truth does not take place in a vacuum, but as part of
Christianity's living with history and its developments. Once this
is admitted, Christianity acknowledges its dependence on historical
contingency in addition to God's revelation of his will and purposes. It is this dependence on history which alerts us to the question of what is true in religion, and leaves us puzzling about what
belongs to God and what belongs to the vicissitudes of history and
culture in the apprehension of religious truth. To raise this distinction at all as something to be taken seriously is itself an indication
of the climate within which theology must now be undertaken and
which was not an issue for generations before the Enlightenment,
at least in its modern acute form. Exclusivism has no answer to the
questions raised by epistemological considerations or the new
historical perspective. This is evident in the fact that the positions
we have outlined either refuse to engage in the debate with philosophy or history, or they severely limit the application of insights
from these disciplines for theological method. The shortcomings
of the exclusivist approach are probably best considered in respect
of the debate with history. Barth answered the questions of history
by saying that all belonged to God in the apprehension of religious

truth, and history plays a minor part, if a part at all. Brunner, Kraemer and Newbigin allowed the historical method to play a less subordinate role, but they harnessed it to the *sola fide* assumption of the Reformation. Historical study therefore challenges the exclusivist theory from two perspectives. First, the conditioned nature of knowledge and religious response implies that any claim by one faith to absoluteness will always appear arbitrary. Second, the particular interpretations of the New Testament and the person of Christ which the exclusivists tend to assume are not the only possible interpretations. This second point is particularly relevant in regard to the debate over the Incarnation. If the response to this criticism is that exclusivism is the only legitimate form of a Christian theology of religions which would preserve a hold on truth in religion (see the quotation from Kraemer, above p. 11), then I would reply that this can only be maintained at the price of a dishonest reckoning with history.

3

INCLUSIVISM

Inclusivism in the Christian theology of religions is both an acceptance and a rejection of the other faiths, a dialectical 'yes' and 'no'.
On the one hand it accepts the spiritual power and depth manifest
in them, so that they can properly be called a locus of divine
presence. On the other hand, it rejects them as not being sufficient
for salvation apart from Christ, for Christ alone is saviour. To be
inclusive is to believe that all non-Christian religious truth belongs
ultimately to Christ and the way of discipleship which springs from
him. Inclusivism therefore involves its adherents in the task of
delineating lines between the Christian faith and the inner religious dynamism of the other faiths. The connections between the
Christian and other faiths are established in a number of different
ways by different writers; yet all see the task as an integral part of
the inclusivist approach. In this respect it is an approach different from the dialectical method of Emil Brunner and Hendrik
Kraemer, whose theology of religions resulted ultimately in the
confrontation of the religions by the Christian message. Inclusivism avoids confrontation, but seeks to discern ways by which the
non-Christian faiths may be integrated creatively into Christian
theological reflection. That is to say, it aims to hold together two
equally binding convictions: the operation of the grace of God in
all the great religions of the world working for salvation, and the
uniqueness of the manifestation of the grace of God in Christ,
which makes a universal claim as the final way of salvation. Though
it is impossible to discover any clear or consistent theory, inclusivism has a pedigree stretching back to the earliest roots of the
Christian tradition. Thus it represents a strand in Christian history

opposed to the dominant influence of exclusivism. Inevitably, in the present encounter between the faiths, the tendencies towards an inclusivist view, largely dormant in the tradition, are being drawn upon as part of the legitimate evidence and justification for this approach as a contemporary possibility. Still, there is no one final shape to the theory. Even in the aftermath of the Second Vatican Council, which undoubtedly gave the greatest impetus to an inclusivist theology of religions, there has been no single line of development. The present chapter examines the inclusivist theory in the Christian theology of religions as it is traced in the Christian tradition and shaped in current debate from a number of different perspectives. Since the Second Vatican Council, Catholic writing on the subject has been prolific, and we shall be concerned, in the major part, with this response. Inclusivism, however, is not the sole prerogative of the Catholic Church; it also occurs in the Orthodox and Protestant traditions. But we shall begin with a brief consideration of the theology of Luke-Acts (viewed as a single corpus), the author of which incorporated his Jewish heritage into his Christian experience in a more thoroughly inclusivist manner than New Testament writers before him. It is instructive to note how he achieves this critical integration, for many of the characteristic elements of some current inclusivist theories are already present at this early stage.

The Acts of the Apostles is a fruitful source for those who seek New Testament backing for a more positive and inclusivist appreciation of the operation of God's Spirit outside Christianity. In the Cornelius narrative Peter says, 'Truly I perceive that God shows no partiality, but in every nation any one who fears him and does what is right is acceptable to him' (10.35). At Lystra, Paul and Barnabas announce to an excited multitude, 'In past generations he allowed all the nations to walk in their own ways; yet he did not leave himself without witness ...' (14.16f.). The inclusivist aspects, however, become more explicit in, for example, Paul's speech on the Areopagus. In this passage (17.22–31) Paul acknowledges the authenticity of the worship of the men of Athens at their altar 'to an unknown God', but goes on to proclaim his identity in terms of the man Jesus, whose resurrection is an assurance that God has appointed him to judge the world. Paul therefore includes the impressive spiritual life of the men of Athens in the Christian way of salvation by conferring a name on the God whom they already worshipped but did not truly recognize. By being so included, their religion was simultaneously brought to completion and perfected. Another way of expressing the same theology is to say that the men of Athens had been Christians without knowing the fact.

The point has often been made that these kinds of passages in Acts provide a convenient contrast to the less generous Paul of the Epistles, or the more exclusivist 'feel' of the New Testament as a whole. The point is worth making, and, as far as it goes, can be accepted. However, a profounder perspective arises if one accepts the assumption of some New Testament scholars that the evangelists were not only handing on given material from the recent past, but also shaped their material towards certain theological ends and according to particular theological presuppositions. If this is granted, then it is possible to place these isolated passages within a wider context deriving from the author's particular theological standpoint. Viewed through the eyes of Luke, it is possible to say that they fittingly reflect the theological outlook of one who was inclusivist in relation to his own Jewish religious past. Of course, all the New Testament writers saw Christianity as superseding the Judaic way, and demonstrated that it was so by various arguments. But, concerned to provide the new Christian way with a venerable past and a possible future in the Roman Empire, Luke was the first to proclaim his gospel in terms of a story set firmly in history. Yet it is probably better to say 'history', for Luke's conception of the term was vastly different from its modern counterpart. History was for him the stage for the providential activity of God, an activity which was not merely stamped on the surface of history but was woven into its very fabric. Moreover, Luke saw this providential activity reaching a culmination point in the life of Jesus. And he did so in two senses which betray his inclusivist methodology. First, the more perfect example of Jesus' life surpassed the piety of any of the Jewish saints and heroes of the past, and it was therefore the touchstone of the fulfilment of the Jewish heritage (Luke 4.21 ; 24.27). As a matter of fact the prophecies of the Jewish past had been completed in the historical life of Jesus. Second, this providential ordering of human affairs not only applies to the Jewish community since Abraham (cf. Matthew's genealogy), but also extends back to the creation of 'Adam, son of God' (Luke 3.38), thus symbolically embracing all human history within its sweep. The genealogy of Jesus in Luke has this significance: Jesus is the fulfilment of all of God's dealings with humanity, since the beginning of history. God has never been absent from the human stage, but has always been preparing it for the coming of Jesus who, as the Christ, becomes the 'centre' of history itself and the clue to its meaning. In this scheme the history of Jesus, and the church which springs from him, become the definitive locus of the providential activity of God in history. Set in this context, therefore, the selected references from the Acts of the Apostles, often cited in support of a Christian inclusivist theology of religions, carry conviction not as isolated texts, but as part of a whole theological outlook which could be said to be inclusivist in tendency. The central ideas of Luke, mainly that Jesus is the culmination of God's providential activity in history, reappear in later inclusivist theories, and are to some extent a foundation for them.

Obviously Luke was not interested in a theology of religions as it strikes the modern theologian, and we must beware of reading him anachronistically. Nevertheless, there is a sense in which the theological outlook of Luke-Acts is analogous to some current inclusivist views. Both are concerned with the place of Christianity in history, and both ask this question in the light of new knowledge. Luke asked it in the light of the knowledge that the expected end of the world was receding and seemed to have been postponed until some unknown time in the future. Current inclusivist theories consider the place of Christianity in history in the knowledge that it is a relatively late phenomenon in the history of the world religions. Yet even before we consider some modern inclusivist positions, it is possible to point out an ambiguity at the heart of the resemblances between the two views, and it turns on the difference in the historical perspective endorsed by them. Given the new knowledge of the history of religions, Hans Küng has posed the problem of historical perspective in the following way:

> In this light the question the Church Fathers used to ask, 'Why did Christ come so late?' has taken on a directness of an entirely new kind.[1]

On the one hand, the resemblances between the ancient and modern views could be interpreted to mean that the current inclusivist theories are wholly within accepted Christian tradition, and represent extensions of that view first outlined by Luke. On the other hand, it could mean that Küng's question has not been answered sufficiently and the new knowledge demands more than an extension of an old theory. We shall return to this point about the ambiguity of the similarity between the ancient and modern views when we have considered modern inclusivism in more detail.

Luke-Acts reflects an author thoroughly steeped in the Jewish tradition, and his inclusivist traits are, in the main, related only to this tradition. Apart from tracing the genealogy of Jesus back to 'Adam, son of God', the theme of world history is mentioned in the Areopagus speech, though it is not developed conceptually. The implications of the speech, however, that Jesus may be relevant to world history, which includes traditions other than the Judaeo-Christian, only become pressing concerns when Christianity shifts from a Jewish to a Hellenistic setting. In this environment the inclusivist 'hints' of the Acts of the Apostles are made more explicit in the Logos theology of the second and third centuries. Justin Martyr, who according to some scholars was of roughly the same period as Luke,[2] is often cited as representative of this style of apologetics. With regard to the operation of the grace of God outside Christianity Justin writes:

> It is our belief that those men who strive to do the good which is enjoined on us have a share in God; according to our traditional belief they will by God's grace share his dwelling. And it is our conviction that this holds good in principle for all men.

For this tradition there is no goodness or truth in the world independent of its origins in the being and action of God. In line with Stoic philosophy Justin believes that all men participate in the universal cosmic Reason, the eternal divine Logos, which is the principle of coherent rationality permeating the basic reality of the universe as a whole, by virtue of the *logos spermatikos* dwelling in their own intrinsic rationality. However, Justin does not confine himself to this general belief, but combines it with his specifically Christian belief which identifies Christ with the divine Logos. Consequently, the above passage continues:

Christ is the divine Word in whom the whole human race share, and those who live according to the light of their knowledge are Christians, even if they are considered as being godless.[3]

Already, therefore, at this early stage, the foundations were being laid for the kind of Christian theology of religions advocated by some post-Vatican II theologians, and in particular, the 'anonymous Christianity' theory of Karl Rahner. The identification of Jesus with the Logos was the key shift which enabled Justin to include the religious life of mankind within the Christian dispensation. Jesus is saviour not only of the Jews and Christians but also of the Gentiles in their own religion. What was for Luke merely a proclamation is now for Justin a part of the Christian philosophy of history. The implications of the identification of Jesus with the Logos are that whatever truth and goodness may be discerned in the non-Christian faiths are partial and incomplete compared with the fullness of truth and goodness which has been given in Christ.

Another way of expressing the same conviction was for the early Apologists to say that mankind was undergoing a process of education in preparation for the appearance of the Logos in Christ. Greek philosophy has acted as a school master (*paedagogos*) in the education of minds to dispose them towards Christ. Clement of Alexandria, for example, could speak of Greek philosophy as 'a stepping-stone leading towards the philosophy of Christ' (*Stromata* 6, 8), and that it 'was given to the Greeks as their Testament' (*Stromata* 5, 8.3). The process of education therefore was not a function of natural thought alone, but was sanctioned as the work of the Holy Spirit of God. Moreover, this was possible since philosophy and theology were not wholly separate disciplines; indeed the work of philosophy in this period was a deeply religious endeavour. Finally, it is worth recalling that Clement viewed the ancient thought and enlightenment of the Indian philosophers, the Brahmans, and the followers of Buddha as more authentic guides and teachers than some of the Greek philosophers to orientate the nations to Christ. This amounts to an affirmation, by Clement, of the presence of divine truth in the religious traditions of the East and, therefore, their assignment to a positive place in the history of salvation.

Both of these notions, the partial revelation granted to other faiths and the presence of the Spirit of God to teach or prepare other faiths to receive the gospel, are paralleled in the Vatican II documents. The *Declaration on the Relation of the Church to Non-Christian Religions (Nostra Aetate)* states:

> The Catholic Church rejects nothing of what is true and holy in these religions. She has a high regard for the manner of life and conduct, the precepts and doctrines which, although differing in many ways from her own teaching, nevertheless often reflect a ray of that truth which enlightens all men.[4]

However, it is necessary in a climate where 'the Church examines with greater care the relation which she has to non-Christian religions',[5] to balance the new openness with an equally obligatory stress on the uniqueness of Christ as universal saviour. The above passage which praises the true and holy in other religions continues:

> Yet she proclaims and is in duty bound to proclaim without fail, Christ who is the way, the truth, and the life (Jn 14.6). In him, in whom God reconciled all things to himself (2 Cor. 5. 18f.), men find the fulness of their religious life.[6]

There is nothing here which goes beyond the earlier quotation from Justin Martyr. The second of the Fathers' themes, the notion of 'preparation', is stated explicitly in the document the *Dogmatic Constitution on the Church (Lumen Gentium)*:

> Those who, through no fault of their own, do not know the Gospel of Christ or his Church, but who nevertheless seek God with a sincere heart, and, moved by grace, try in their actions to do his will as they know it through the dictates of their conscience – those too may achieve eternal salvation . . .
>
> Whatever good or truth is found amongst them is considered by the Church to be a preparation for the Gospel and given by him who enlightens all men that they may at length have life.[7]

Again, in the words of the *Decree on the Church's Missionary Activity (Ad Gentes Divinitus)*, though they require healing and illumination by Christ, the religious endeavours of men 'may lead one to the true God and be a preparation for the Gospel'.[8]

As official statements by the Roman Catholic Church the documents of Vatican II do not submit a detailed theory of the relation between Christianity and the other faiths. Their role in Catholic theology has been to signal a change from exclusivism to inclusivism in the approach to the other faiths at a fundamental theological level. The older Catholic attitude began with the dogma that there is 'no salvation outside the church' (*Extra Ecclesiam nulla salus*). The newer approach begins with a consideration of the will and mind of God for the whole world as this has been made known in the biblical revelation. Hans Küng has termed this a shift from an ecclesiocentric to a theocentric view.[9] If the Second Vatican Council represents a landmark in this respect in the history of Christian theology, it is one which nevertheless makes an appeal to an older, though neglected, area of concern in the writings of the Fathers. All the recent statements of a Christian theology of religions from Catholic writers, stimulated by the new openness of the Council, claim a pedigree in the early centuries of Christian theology.

The major architect of the post-conciliar Catholic contribution to the subject is undoubtedly Karl Rahner. In an address entitled 'Christianity and the Non-Christian Religions', given in 1964, Rahner proposed four theses as an outline towards a Christian theology of religions. It is worth relaying these in some detail, not least because of the vigorous debate which this authoritative Catholic writer has initiated. The first thesis defines the starting-point:

> ... Christianity understands itself as the absolute religion, intended for all men, which cannot recognize any other religion beside itself as of equal right.[10]

On parallel with the theology of Karl Barth, this proposition derives from the basic conviction that God has freely and finally communicated himself in his revelation in Christ. But for Rahner this christological affirmation does not limit salvation to those who have responded to the revelation in Christ. What it affirms is that salvation, wherever it may be said to be present, is always of Christ, for Christ alone is saviour. Salvation is always Christian salvation because this is the meaning and definition God has chosen to give it by virtue of the Incarnation. This leaves open an inclusive understanding of the place of non-Christian religions in the economy and activity of God's salvific purposes for the world. For, in addition to declaring definitively his purposes in Christ, God also 'desires all men to be saved and to come to the knowledge of the truth' (I Tim. 2.4). This second dogmatic principle leads to Rahner's second thesis:

> Until the moment when the gospel really enters into the historical situation of an individual, a non-Christian religion . . . does not merely contain elements of a natural knowledge of God, elements, moreover, mixed up with human depravity . . . It contains also supernatural elements arising out of the grace which is given . . . on account of Christ. For this reason a non-Christian religion can be recognized as a lawful religion . . .[11]

By lawful religion Rahner means one which can be counted as having positive significance as a means for achieving salvation and a right relationship with God.

This second thesis needs to be understood from the point of view of Rahner's interpretation of the relation between nature and grace, and his doctrine of man. Nature and grace do not describe entirely separate and distinct phases in the historic life of the individual or community. When a person hears the gospel call he does not hear it as a natural creature *per se*, but as one already 'graced', that is, already ordered towards the Spirit of God, the acceptance of which is simultaneously the completion of a person's humanity and is therefore his salvation. This doctrine that man's supernatural goal 'stamps' or 'determines' his nature before it is freely accepted is termed by Rahner the 'supernatural existential'.[12] He expresses the same notion when he says that man is created 'a being of unlimited openness for the limitless being of God',[13] and in the acceptance of his unlimited openness he can be said to be already living a spiritual existence. When this is linked with the christological belief that man's supernatural goal has been freely expressed in the life of Christ, the implications for a Christian theology of religions become clearer:

> In the acceptance of himself man is accepting Christ as the absolute perfection and guarantee of his own anonymous movement towards God by grace, and the acceptance of this belief is

46

again not an act of man alone but the work of God's grace which is the grace of Christ . . .[14]

Grace, therefore, is operative in a person's life in his awareness of himself as an open being of unlimited potential, and it is operative prior to any conscious acceptance of the gospel. But Rahner's second thesis goes further than its foundation in his doctrine of man, nature and grace, and states that the grace of God operates to qualify a non-Christian *religion* as a vehicle of salvation. Whenever expression is given in sacred rites and scriptures to the experienced relationship between man and God, the grace of God can be said to be operating anonymously within the religion itself working for salvation. The justification for this step in the argument derives from the observation that religion is necessarily social in nature. Personal life implies individual involvement in society with others. To conceive that individuals could be saved apart from the institutions which mediate the saving relationship would be to conceive of the individual as a non-historical and non-social being. Non-Christian religions can therefore be said to be vehicles of salvation, available to individuals in their particular and differing historical settings, and given by God for the purposes of achieving the saving relationship.

If the non-Christian religions are legitimate or lawful religions in God's plan of salvation, what then is the relationship between Christianity and the other religions? Rahner points to the answer in his third thesis:

. . . Christianity does not simply confront the members of an extra-Christian religion as a mere non-Christian but as someone who can and must already be regarded in this or that respect as an anonymous Christian.[15]

Reminiscent of Paul's speech on the Areopagus, the difference between Christianity and the other faiths is that Christians claim to name the reality which is anonymously present in the other faiths and operative in their rites and ceremonies for salvation. In a specific study of the relationship between Hinduism and Christianity, Raymond Panikkar has expressed this theory of 'anonymous Christianity' in the following way:

The good and *bona fide* Hindu is saved by Christ and not by

Hinduism, but it is through the Sacraments of Hinduism, through the *Mysterion* that comes to him through Hinduism, that *Christ* saves the Hindu normally.[16]

One difficulty with this view is that of identifying Christ's presence in the Hindu sacraments, or how he saves through them. Presumably, it is only in a general sense, that is, by virtue of the spiritual and moral principles inherent in the Hindu way as a whole, that Christ can be said to be present. But the justification for the theory is not offered on the basis of a detailed account of the beliefs and practices of Christians and Hindus. It is a matter of dogmatic theology, and represents the outcome of a tradition which attempts to hold in tension two equally binding convictions – the universal will of God to save and the unique role of Christ as saviour. Inevitably it leads to a re-evaluation of the church's mission, which traditionally tended to approach non-Christian peoples as living outside the sphere of God's gracious care and activity. Re-evaluation of the missionary task demands re-evaluation of the church's understanding of itself *vis-à-vis* the other faiths. Rahner defines the constitution of the church in his fourth thesis as the

> historically tangible vanguard and the historically and socially constituted explicit expression of what the Christian hopes is present as a hidden reality even outside the visible Church.[17]

On this basis the Christian mission is to witness before the world faiths to the mystery of Christ who works, hidden and unperceived, within their rituals and institutions. The church is not the exclusive club of salvation; rather, it is the conscious embodiment of the salvific power of Christ, which has always been active in the world even before the Incarnation. It is an inclusivist understanding of the church which was, again, pursued by the early Fathers. Augustine, for example, affirmed that Christ was universally present and influential before the Incarnation, a notion which led him to say that the church itself had existed before Christ's coming in the flesh. In his famous doctrine '*Ecclesia a Justo Abel*', Augustine said that Abel was the first just man, and that every just man after him belonged to Christ and the church. In this sense Rahner's belief that 'somehow all men must be capable of being members of the Church'[18] had already been prefigured by Augustine. But this does not alter the necessity for the church's missionary work. Mission is still a command laid on the church by its Lord. Its task is to bring to explicit consciousness the gift of grace which has been accepted implicitly. Writing as a missionary, Eugene Hillman has expressed why mission is an integral part of the Christian work:

> The point is that the Church must be raised up among enough of the peoples to symbolize adequately the real presence of Christ among all men in every part of the world.[19]

Such a re-evaluation of the church's mission is a direct outcome of Rahner's theory of 'anonymous Christianity', and Hillman acknowledges his dependence on Rahner. The old doctrine, 'outside the Church no salvation', has been retained, though in radically reinterpreted form.

On this question of the church's missionary task there are parallels with the more exclusivist theology of Karl Barth. For example, Küng, in an address given in 1964, makes a comparable statement to Barth's reference to the future when speaking of what men of other faiths have it in them to become (see above, p. 15):

> Whilst well aware of the distance and alienation from God of the people in the world religions, she (the Church) does not appeal to them in terms of that past state of estrangement which Christ has *brought to a close*, but in terms of the future which Christ has opened up.[20]

Or, again, Küng echoes Barth when he draws out the implications of the future which Christ has opened up, for our understanding of ecclesiology:

> The Church is thus the sign inviting the peoples of the world religions, so that from being Christians *de iure* they may become Christians *de facto*, from Christians *in spe* to Christians *in re*; that from being Christians by designation and vocation, they may become Christians by profession and witness.[21]

Barth, of course, would not assent to the theorizing which lay behind Küng's application of the terms 'Christians *de iure*' and 'Christians *in spe*' to the peoples of the non-Christian faiths. Parallels between Barth and Küng break down at this level.

Although Küng was later to change his mind (we shall discuss Küng's more recent contribution, in his *On Being a Christian*, below), at this stage he was in substantial agreement with Rahner, and distinguishes between 'ordinary' and 'extraordinary' ways of salvation. The former is operative in general salvation history for the non-Christian peoples of the world, and the latter is operative in the church for Christian salvation. Undoubtedly, Barth would have rejected this as compromising the newness of the gospel. However, it was not the intention of Küng's inclusivism to ignore the newness of the gospel or the necessity for conversion. Conscious and explicit profession of Christian salvation involves more than merely a question of 'gnosis', that is, the reception by adherents of other faiths of spiritual knowledge from otherwise enlightened Christians. Küng does argue that becoming Christian 'by profession and witness', from being Christian 'by designation and vocation', also involves conversion and invitation to a new level of witness in the unfolding of salvation history. Whether this is compatible with the principles inherent in the theses of Rahner is a moot point. Certainly it has precipitated a great deal of debate; and we shall return to it below.

Rahner's theory has persisted in more or less original form since its first enunciation in 1961 to the most recent defence in Volume 16 of his *Theological Investigations*. We have considered it in detail because it has come to represent an authoritative statement from within contemporary Catholic debate on the subject. However, this line of development is not confined to Catholic theologians; a recent statement from within the Orthodox Church shows a substantially similar argument. In an address given in 1971 at the Central Committee Meeting of the WCC, Metropolitan Georges Khodr spoke of the hidden Christ within other religious traditions:

> Christ is hidden everywhere in the mystery of his lowliness. Any reading of religions is a reading of Christ. It is Christ alone who is received as light when grace visits a Brahmin, a Buddhist or a Muhammadan reading his own scriptures.[22]

The background theology for this Orthodox version of inclusivism lies in the doctrine of the Holy Spirit who operates in the world distinctly from the Son, filling all things. Khodr can therefore say, 'All who are visited by the Spirit are the people of God.'[23] Other faiths can be said to derive from the same Spirit of God. The Spirit, however, is also the bridge between the Incarnation and the other faiths, working in them to fashion the presence of Christ at their heart. Only with the Christian church has this process reached explicit expression, and it constitutes the difference between the Christian and other faiths. As with Rahner, the relationship between Christianity and the other faiths is that of complete to incomplete, explicit to implicit, open to anonymous.

These statements of an inclusivist theology of religions from within the Catholic and Orthodox traditions are not intended to be exhaustive, yet they may be accepted as representative of the kind of exploration which is currently being undertaken. Though the thrust of the argument is substantially the same for both communities, there are differences in the method of approach to Christian theology itself, differences which have particular consequences in the Christian theology of religions. Because of the Orthodox stress on the apophatic method and their sense of the unknowability of God, it is difficult to discern anything which may be said to be definitive in the Christian theology of religions from that community. On the other hand, the Catholic stress on conciliar statements defined by the magisterium leads to a clearer statement about what might be termed a Catholic point of view, and consequently it is easier to trace the effects of the conciliar statement in different theologians. Karl Rahner's influence in this field has been widespread and can be traced in a number of writers concerned with the question both in dogmatic theology and from the perspective of the missionary endeavour of the church. I have already cited Eugene Hillman as an example of Rahner's influence on a missionary theologian; an example in the realm of dogmatic theology can be seen in the work of Heinz Robert Schlette. It is worth outlining Schlette's analysis not least because it bears the strongest resemblance to the central features of the theological outlook of Luke-Acts, and claims a basis which is both biblical and critical-historical.

Schlette conceives his inclusivism in terms of 'salvation history', a concept which signifies the unfolding of the revelation of God at particular times and stages in the history of the world. A distinction is made between *general* and *special* sacred history, both of which lead to the correlative terms *ordinary* and *extraordinary* ways

51

of salvation as descriptions of the life of faith in the non-Christian and Christian religions respectively. The distinction has a strong basis in the biblical account of the two covenants specified in Genesis. General sacred history points to the covenant made between God and the whole of humanity through Noah (Gen. 8.20–9.17); special sacred history points to the covenant between God and Israel, beginning with Abraham and reaching fruition in Christ and his church. The first covenant ensures that non-Christian response to God's desire that the whole world be saved is genuine response:

> If general sacred history can and must be held to be positively willed by God, then non-Christian religions also have to be considered to be willed and sanctioned by God.[24]

This is not meant to imply that Christianity and all other religions exist on an equal footing. What is being claimed is simply that Christianity does not have a monopoly of the means of salvation. For to affirm that all religions are equal ways of salvation would be a denial, on this view, of the grace and knowledge of God freely given by way of special sacred history in Israel, Christ and the church. Hence:

> Christianity's superiority is not a judgement made out of arrogance but is affirmed solely because it pleased God to reveal his glory and at the same time the mystery of history by the incomparable way of special sacred history . . . because God can act as seems good to him.[25]

Faith in the free act of God in Jesus Christ stands therefore as the foundation on which the Christian way becomes the final goal of the religious endeavours of mankind. Special sacred history is related to ordinary sacred history not as truth is to falsehood, but as complete to incomplete, perfect to imperfect, plant to seed. The Christian faith that God has acted as seems good to him leads to distinction in the unfolding of salvation history, but not to total differentiation. Close relationship exists between the two ways of salvation 'in having a common origin, meaning and goal and being subject to the same grace of God'.[26] As we have noted above (pp. 40ff.), this balance between uniqueness and continuity in the action of God's grace through history was first achieved by Luke, the original author of 'salvation history'. Schlette's scheme is a development of the same style of theology. But we also noted an ambiguity surrounding the similarities between the ancient and the modern view. The question remains: does the new historical consciousness, developed over the last 200 years, and the concomitant knowledge of mankind's varied religious life, warrant more than an extension of an old theory? This leads us to a consideration of some of the objections against inclusivism as a viable solution to the problem of a Christian theology of religions.

In spite of the declarations of the Second Vatican Council and the authoritative power of a writer like Rahner, the inclusivist theory of 'anonymous Christianity' has not been without its opponents from both inside and outside the Catholic allegiance. From inside, the main line of objection concerns the significance given to the Incarnation in the theory as a whole. It is claimed that this has been undermined in two ways: by lessening the necessity for conversion, and by the acceptance of the other faiths as genuine vehicles of salvation. It is permissible to grant that the grace of God is present in the lives of individual non-Christians as the source of all their inspiration, operating for their salvation; every sincere religious man who responds generously to God's calling is saved by Christ who dwells secretly in the heart. But it is claimed that to extend this to institutional non-Christian religion is tantamount to denying the newness of the gospel. One opponent of Rahner, Henri de Lubac, defends the uniqueness of the Christian way in the following terms:

> Even if not formally contradicting one another, if several ways of salvation really exist, parallel in some manner, then we are faced with a great dispersal, not a spiritual convergence . . . if we aspire to unity, then we have no choice but to search for an axis, a drawing and unifying force which is the Spirit of the Lord animating the Church.[27]

The unity of God's will of salvation for the world demands a single axis or focus if it is to mean anything at all. Christianity does indeed 'fulfil' the world's religious quest, but in a way which first demands the death of the other traditions so that what is noble, good and true in them can rise up and establish a place in Christianity. For the opponents of 'anonymous Christianity', then, the cost of the new Vatican II openness is too great because it loosens a hold on the uniqueness of Christ. In practice it would appear that there is no considerable difference between the faiths in terms of their role as means of salvation in the divine intention for the world.

Inclusivism proceeds on the basis of commitment to two equally binding convictions: the universal will of God to save, and the uniqueness of the revelation in Christ. The internal debate among Catholic writers raises the question whether it is possible to hold these two principles in tension for a coherent Christian theology of religions. It appears that different convictions are emphasized by the two sides in the debate. Rahner, Schlette, Panikkar and others emphasize the continuity in God's universal will to save, blurring the boundary between the Christian and other faiths with the consequence that between an anonymous encounter with Christ and open recognition there is no more than a process of self-awakening. De Lubac and others emphasize the need for conversion to Christ and his church if justice is to be done to the newness of salvation which Christ brings. Now it is the case that theology often proceeds by holding in tension convictions which point in opposite directions. Examples of this are abundant in the doctrines of God (holding together transcendence and immanence), Christ (humanity and divinity), salvation (nature and grace). And certainly there is a sense in which words and descriptions can never exhaust the mystery of the relationship between the Creator and the created. Nevertheless it is incumbent on the theologian to express as clearly and coherently as possible the relationship between his two convictions. It may be that his theory lacks any real content if it cannot be stated coherently. Is the tension in these versions of inclusivism strained beyond coherence and viability? Is there an impasse which can be taken as *prima facie* evidence that inclusivism is a wrong method in the Christian theology of religions? Some writers acknowledge the impasse but believe that it is still necessary to seek a coherent statement of the theory. James Dupuis, for example, believes that 'a solution may be found by distinguishing various modalities of the sacramental presence of the Christic mystery'.[28] However, the problem with this kind of solution is to know precisely what the language means. Dupuis himself admits this when later in the same essay he writes:

The words fail us to express adequately the distinction and unity between the cosmic religions and Christianity.[29]

Again, is the failure of words evidence of mystery or intolerable strain? To be fair to the inclusivists, the different emphases which Rahner and de Lubac represent have been present in Christian theology since New Testament times. So far as their concern is with history, the theologies of Luke and of Paul are analogous to the two emphases under discussion. Writing of the theology of Luke, John Drury has said:

> History is no longer, as in Paul, the anvil on which God hammers out salvation at white heat, but the medium in which he is made known in its rhythm of prophecy and fulfilment.[30]

De Lubac (like Paul) is more existential, in that God's dramatic irruption into history demands a decision from the individual to be converted to the new way. Rahner (like Luke) is more concerned to smooth over the blatant discontinuities in God's providential care, showing how God has always been preparing history for the coming of Jesus, who brings final salvation to the whole world. Perhaps there has always been a tension between these two styles of theology in Christian history. The question for today is whether the new knowledge of the history of religions strains the tension beyond a tolerable level, and renders both styles inadequate to deal with it.

Pointing out a *prima facie* objection does no more than suggest the need for a closer examination of a thesis. More serious objections, however, can be raised against theories of 'anonymous Christianity' when they are analysed in a further critical light. The major objection is this: theories of inclusivism impose themselves *a priori* on the world faiths, whose acknowledged salvific value makes no real difference to the shape of one's own theological commitment. There is a sense in which the inclusivist theorising is no more than tautologous. If Jesus Christ is posited as the only true saviour (in other language, the Logos incarnate), and all people in their various faiths have been created orientated towards Christ as their goal and fulfilment (in other language, given a share in the Logos by virtue of the *logos spermatikos* inherent in human nature), then to say that Christ and his church therefore represent the fullness of religion is to do no more than argue in a circle. Maurice Wiles has expressed this objection succinctly:

> If . . . every positive insight must derive from the Logos and, since Jesus was the Logos incarnate, it belongs in a fuller and more fundamental sense to Christ and the religion that acknowledges him, then it is no more than a tautology. On this argument since all good comes from the Logos and Jesus is the Logos incarnate we can know in advance that every good belongs to him, whatever the empirical evidence.[31]

Wiles illustrates his point further with reference to the newer Catholic teaching on the church. In the old view the church was the sole and exclusive place where salvation was known; but now that salvation is not confined to the church, it must be redefined to mean simply all those who respond to the light of truth which has been variously given to all people throughout history. When the concept of church has been stretched beyond any normal definition of the term, one wonders, with Wiles, whether the issue has been pre-judged. The circularity of the argument could also be illustrated with reference to Rahner's doctrine of the 'supernatural existential'. When he says that man is a being whose completion and destiny is to be filled with the grace of Christ it adds nothing to the original premise that the grace of Christ is already operative in a person who accepts himself as spirit. This means that not only adherents of the non-Christian faiths may be regarded as anonymous Christians, but also, as Anita Röper has said, that 'every human being may be regarded as a Christian in one way or another'.[32] This is the logical outcome of the inclusivist theory, and again it is a puzzle to know what meaning to attach to the language. In the Christian theology of religions it means that the relationship between Christianity and the other religions can be known irrespective of the knowledge of those faiths themselves. The issue has been pre-judged, and this line of approach represents a refusal to take seriously the other faiths on their own terms.

 Wiles' complaint is that it is invalid in an age of historical studies to formulate a theology of religions without some recourse to the evidence of the religions themselves. Historical studies have given rise to the need for a Christian theology of religions initially, and it would seem unhistorical if the results of such studies went unheeded in the formulation of the theology itself. Given this historical climate, for inclusivism to gain respect it must be able to delineate the lines of continuity and convergence between Christianity and the other faiths in a way which does not impose Christian categories *a priori*. In this regard, it is interesting to note that the historical requirement has not always been absent from some versions of inclusivism. The best example of a work which included detailed reference to the empirical life of a non-Christian faith, and proceeded according to the historical requirement, was *The Crown of Hinduism* (1913), by the Protestant writer Dr J. N. Farquhar of the Indian YMCA. Here it was advanced that in essence Christ, not Christianity, is the fulfilment of the aspirations and quests revealed in Hindu religious history:

> Christ provides the fulfilment of the highest aspirations of Hinduism . . . In Him is focused every ray of light that shines in Hinduism. He is the Crown of the Faith of India.[33]

Farquhar's work demonstrated a great wealth of learning and knowledge. He believed that his 'fulfilment' theory was not an imposition of Christian categories but truly reflected what was the case after a detailed study of Hindu religious life: not reified 'Hinduism' but Hindu scriptures, family system, asceticism, caste, worship, find their fulfilment in Christ.

Farquhar's theory represents an honest and open attempt to wrestle with Christian revelation and revelation everywhere. It gives the lie to those who think that the church has, until recent times, always set out to confront the other faiths with the exclusive Christian gospel. The impression is often given by Catholic writers that the openness sounded by Vatican II was wholly new in the development of the Christian theology of religions this century. In the rush to print after the Council many writers chose simply not to refer to this previous work by Farquhar, or they were ignorant of it. Yet it does represent a version of inclusivism which was gaining recognition at the beginning of this century. Nevertheless, fulfilment theory, at least in this form, has not survived as a viable Christian theology of religions for two major reasons.

First, Farquhar was strongly influenced by the scholarship current at the beginning of the century, which has now been superseded. The vast knowledge of the religious traditions of the world was being accumulated under the headings 'Science of Religion', 'Comparative Religion', and 'History of Religion', and was arranged according to an evolutionary model of progress. Moreover it was possible to delineate progress in religion along ethical lines, all of which pointed to Christianity as the religion of highest ethical worth. When this was linked with the Christian view of the uniqueness of Christ, it was not hard to avoid the fulfilment conclusion. However, most theologians of the history of religions would not now arrange their material according to an evolutionary model. Religions, we have come to see, are more diverse and variegated than was once assumed, displaying a life which is a complex and culturally-related unity. Although Farquhar showed scholarly awareness of the religious traditions of Hinduism, he often assumed Hinduism to be more of a unity than is really the case.

Second, the fulfilment theory can be said to place too much emphasis on the person of the historical Jesus. That is to say, it comes dangerously close to assuming that Christian faith requires that every non-Christian 'high' moral or religious value must of necessity be reflected in the human life of Christ. Historically this is clearly untenable. It militates against the humanity of Christ, and ignores the distinctive cultural associations which form part of any religious belief. In particular, it means that Jesus becomes the focus of salvation of, say, the Hindu, while ignoring the Hindu diagnosis of the human condition for which salvation is offered. Farquhar did take note of the empirical evidence of Hindu life, but, ultimately he was unable to escape the same kind of imposed *a priori* theories which were to come later after Vatican II. As E. J. Sharpe has noted, there were times when Farquhar's evidence was 'tortured to fit the theory, instead of the theory being shaped to fit all the available evidence'.[34]

There are parallels and similarities between all the versions of inclusivism we have discussed. The notion of fulfilment in some form, for example, is a constant theme. Also the necessity to show some empirical connections between Christianity and the other faiths was a recurrent factor even prior to the present historical climate. Farquhar sensed the requirement to marshal some empirical evidence to substantiate his theory, but he was not an innovator in this respect. The first to do this with any degree of thoroughness was the author of Luke-Acts, who justified the superiority of the new Christian way using prophecy-fulfilment arguments. Jesus not only lived the perfect 'pious' life, important for the whole human race since Adam, but also laid down the example for 'church' life in the future, written up in Acts. The key to human history resides in the life of Jesus himself. Justin Martyr followed the method of prophecy-fulfilment, but added the Logos doctrine to include the Gentile world within the providential preparation for the Christian revelation. The prophecy-fulfilment argument is shown, for example, in his comment, 'This is the deed of God – to tell a thing before it happens, and then to show it happening as foretold' (1 *Apology* 12.10). It was the addition of the Logos doctrine which created the precedent for an *a priori* judgment on the other faiths. Rahner and others represent a new departure not because they attempt to take account of the historical evidence of the religions gathered over the last two hundred years, but because they abandoned the prophecy-fulfilment motif of the Apologists and constructed their theories entirely *a priori*. It is no wonder that the inclusivism of 'anonymous Christianity' appears contrived and a pre-judgment of the issues; for in an age which values historical studies, the links between Christianity and the other religions demand more careful historical attention than in the past, not simply abandonment.

If the major criticism of the recent versions of inclusivism is that they pre-judge the issue, then it is a criticism which must not be directed against all of those who hold the post-conciliar view. There are a number of inclusivists who are not armchair theologians, but who write from the vantage point of many years' experience of living within another culture and religious setting. The most familiar names are Raymond Panikkar, Dom Bede Griffiths, Henri le Saux (Abhishiktananda) and Klaus Klostermaier. All attempt to delineate the points of contact between Christianity and, in these instances, Hinduism, either by replacing the Old Testament with Hindu scriptures as the only appropriate *praeparatio evangelica* in an Indian culture, or by developing an Indian christology which tries to show how Christ is already at work within Hindu thought and faith.

The basic assumption of this group of writers is that the faiths meet, as the Hindu would say, 'in the cave of the heart'. Neither intellectual nor existential approaches can achieve the real meeting which inter-religious dialogue sets out to achieve. In Thomas Merton's words:

> Ecumenism seeks the inner and ultimate spiritual 'ground' which underlies all articulated differences.[35]

In other words, the genuine encounter between faiths can only take place within the mystical or contemplative traditions of the faiths. In this experience the external intellectual frameworks of the faiths are abandoned, for they merely hinder proper exchange in the search for the truth:

> This Truth is to be found beyond all the formulations of the schools and beyond all the revelations of the scriptures, in the inner depths of the heart, beyond words and thoughts, where the divine Word is spoken and the mystery of Being is made known.[36]

Passages of this kind could be multiplied in all these writers. All agree that a Christian theology of religions without the first-hand experience of a 'Return to the Centre' is unwarranted and destined to failure.

Stipulation of the mystical experience as the place of meeting between faiths is not meant to affirm that all faiths are equal or in essence the same, but that God has been revealing himself to all peoples throughout time. The implications of this belief are made by Bede Griffiths in an earlier work:

> These insights, insofar as they each reflect the one Reality, are in principle complementary.[37]

What, however, may be possible in principle turns out in reality to be not the case. To have followed this line of thought would have placed Griffiths in the same fold as the so-called relativists or pluralists. In the end he belongs with the inclusivists when he writes:

> We have to show how Christ is, as it were, 'hidden' at the heart of Hinduism, of Buddhism, of Islam, and how it is the one Word of God which has enlightened mankind from the beginning of history . . .[38]

Such universalist claims arise from the Christian belief in the uniqueness of Christ. At this level, therefore, Griffiths has added nothing from his long experience in India to the 'anonymous Christianity' theory of Rahner. But, unlike Rahner, he does not leave his inclusivism without further argument at this theoretical level. In his work *Vedanta and Christian Faith*, he shows how it is possible to interpret certain trends in the theology of the chief spokesmen of Vedanta as pointing towards the kind of expression which is clearest in Christian doctrine. The main problem turns on the attempt by Hindu writers to understand the relation between God and the material universe. Griffiths believes that the doctrines of God in both Sankara, the classic theologian of Vedanta, and Thomas Aquinas are at root identical, but that in their developed interpretation of the relation between God and the world there is a fundamental difference between the two theologians. Yet Griffiths believes that Hindu theologians have not been content to rest with the classic non-dualism of Sankara, and they have struggled to seek distinctions between the Brahman and the universe, while simultaneously trying to hold on to non-dualism. These later reflections come closer to the Christian view and represent a movement towards it. Consequently, it is possible to view Christian doctrine in some sense as a completion or clarification of the understanding which Hindus have been seeking:

> In the question of the relation between the universe and God, St. Thomas introduced an exact conception of creation which clarifies the eastern tradition, but leaves it essentially unchanged.[39]

It is this kind of argument which forms part of the justification for Griffith's inclusivism, part of the search to find the points of contact between Hinduism and Christianity. But it is to his original assumption that the faiths meet in the 'cave of the heart' that he returns. At the end of his study he comes full circle and affirms that in the ultimate state of unity with God, which is at the same time a transformation into the 'divine darkness' (Dionysius), differences will be transcended and in the final beatific vision 'Hindu and Christian unite not only with one another but also with the Buddhist and the Muslim'.[40]

There is a tension in the theory as depicted by Bede Griffiths between a drive towards complementarity in religious descrpitions of the ineffable truth of the one God and the determining factors of Christian inclusivism. On the whole he confesses inclusivism, but occasionally he appears to follow a pluralist approach. I have chosen Bede Griffiths as an example of the kind of inclusivism which is the result of living Christian faith in an Indian setting, yet a similar understanding could be found in the other writers mentioned above. In all of them three general points form the construction of the theory. First, the assumption that the innermost depths of the believing heart, beyond intellect and sense, is the true locus for an encounter between religions. Second, there is assent to the belief that the religions 'all alike are conditioned by history and circumstance, but all derive from the one Source and all alike point to the one Reality'.[41] Third, in view of the Incarnation, 'nothing can remain outside Christ or be independent of his Headship',[42] so that the position finally adopted is thoroughly inclusivist. In spite of the sometimes very detailed attempt to show theologically how the Hindu may discover the goal of his spiritual quest in the Christian faith, the second and third points above remain in uneasy tension. It is the same unease found between Rahner's first and second theses, which point in opposite directions. The criticism that inclusivism pre-judges the issue of truth in religion is still relevant and pertinent.

If pre-judging constitutes the major criticism of the inclusivist theory, because it is held to be inconsistent with an age of historical studies, this is not to say that it has not adjusted to some of the challenges arising from the critical historical consciousness. One of the key distinctions which such an age has forced on Christian theology is that between truth and salvation. It is a theoretical distinction which enables the inclusivist to formulate a two-tiered understanding of salvation as, for example, between ordinary and extraordinary ways of salvation, or anonymous Christians and fully-fledged Christians. Certainly I believe there can be no going back on this distinction, yet the way in which it is worked out in these theories does foreclose the question of truth. Moreover, it renders dialogue a meaningless encounter, for the Christian would have nothing, essentially, to learn from his non-Christian partner. In this respect Hans Küng has scathingly criticized these versions of inclusivist theories:

This is a pseudo-solution which offers slight consolation. Is it possible to cure a society suffering from a decline in membership by declaring that even non-members are 'hidden' members?[43]

The question arises whether it is possible to sustain the distinction between truth and salvation without falling into a relativism which regards every religious expression as being equally good or true. In other words, is there an inclusivism which respects and acknowledges the truth of other faiths, does not pre-judge them, and remains open to the exploration of unknown truth in dialogue? Two writers from very different backgrounds, Hans Küng and John Robinson, have answered this question in the affirmative and their contributions deserve careful appraisal. We shall consider them in turn.

Küng has written of Christianity as possessing the potential for a critical synthesis of religious truths:

> Could not therefore all that which otherwise exists perhaps isolated and scattered, fragmentarily and sporadically, distorted and disfigured, be brought to its full realisation in Christianity: without a false, antithetic exclusiveness, but with a creative rethinking, resulting in a new, inclusive and simultaneously critical synthesis?[44]

It will be clear that this is an inclusivism which does not impose Christianity on the adherents of other faiths but proceeds by listening and respecting the insights and theological truths expressed in their faiths. The dialogue, which Küng believes to be the foundation for establishing a critical synthesis, contains a number of tensions. It would be an encounter where the non-Christian faiths would be encouraged to bring out what is best in them, where the truth embodied in them would be respected, but the Christian faith would neither be compromised nor reduced to general truths. There would be a mutual critical questioning: Christianity would have things to learn from the other faiths as well as submitting its own apprehension of religious truth before them. Finally, Küng specifies that there would be a common quest for truth; and the tension here is that each faith is bound by its own tradition, but ought to be open to new perceptions of truth as a result of the contacts between the faiths.

How is Küng's version of inclusivism to be assessed? The question which faces us is whether the tensions involved in his 'inclusive and simultaneously critical synthesis' are more acceptable than the intolerable strains of the inclusivism we outlined above, and the earlier convictions of Küng himself. The elements of mutual questioning and a common search for truth in his theory suggest that the one God is known variously throughout the religious traditions of the world according to different cultural and philosophical concepts. But the notion that there is no differentiation in truth between faiths is anathema to Küng. The question remains: by what criteria are we to specify the truth in religion? For Rahner the answer was given *a priori*: Christ hidden within the traditions of the other faiths. For Küng, the criteria are ostensibly left to be worked out in the dialogue. Nevertheless the impression is that he views Christianity as the final arbiter of religious truth. Christianity has at least the potential for including within its outlook and confession of faith the insights and theological truths contained in the other faiths. This may indeed be so, but one wonders, when Küng so readily sees dialogue as essential for inter-religious reckoning with truth, whether his conclusion is premature. What does a mutual quest for truth mean when Christianity is submitted as the locus for the 'full realization' of religious truth fragmented among the religious traditions of the world? Clearly problems remain, even with Küng's revised version of inclusivism.

The other writer we have mentioned who has independently constructed a Christian theology of religions remarkably similar to Küng's inclusivism in its essential nature is John Robinson. He is worth consideration alongside Küng not only because his background in Protestant Christianity differs from Küng's Catholic inheritance, but also because he makes more explicit than Küng the christological components of his argument.

As the title of Robinson's book suggests, in religion 'truth is two-eyed'. Indeed he avows that it is many-eyed, but for the purposes of this particular study he confines the discussion to the dialogue between two centres of religious experience, broadly speaking the prophetic and the mystic, both of which occur in any one religious tradition but are separately writ large as clusters of ideas and practices in the traditions of East and West. Yet underlying these two dominant types of religious experience it is possible to speak of God as one:

> The God who discloses himself in Jesus and the God who dis-
> closes himself in Krishna must be the same God, or he is no
> God – and there is no revelation at all. *Ultimately* for both sides
> there are not 'gods many and lords many' but one God, under
> whatever name . . .[45]

Matters of religious truth are best pursued along lines which hold
the predominant centres in a creative tension, which both respects
important differences and yet rejects isolation as a distortion.
Robinson shows how this creative tension is currently being explored in relation to the themes of the 'historical' and the 'material'.
The method he adopts to demonstrate that 'truth is two-eyed' is to
consider how each centre has moved away from an exclusive one-
eyed view towards more recognition of the validity of the other
centre's view; then in a kind of negative argument he shows how
each centre's one-eyed view, when pressed to its limits, leads to a
serious distortion even of its own truth. It is worth citing Robinson
at length to illustrate more clearly his method. So, for example, in
relation to the historical, the East has shown signs of acknowledg-
ing a Western emphasis:

> I found Hindus wishing to stress that history was processive
> and spiral rather than purely cyclical and to claim that, unlike
> Christians, they believed in an open system with no final term.
> Even in those who have laid most emphasis on timelessness
> there is a perceptible shift of emphasis.[46]

And the West has shown signs of embodying an Eastern emphasis:

> In all the recent turning towards Eastern religions, meditation
> and yoga there is a distinct turning away from any kind of
> exclusive historical claims or Protestant particularism, and in
> the renewed awareness, especially through Jungian psychology,
> of the importance of myth and archetype there is a new readiness
> to detach the Christ-figure from more than a minimal depen-
> dence on the Jesus of history.[47]

In the second stage of the argument Robinson then notes the distortion of a one-eyed view when pressed to its limits. In respect of
the West:

On the one hand, we have a historical positivism or funda-
mentalism of an all-or-nothing kind, which lacks discrimination,
self-criticism and above all imagination.[48]

Then:

On the other hand, the East at its worst . . . has been characterized by a dangerous historical absenteeism, making for a
quietist indifference and fatalistic irresponsibility.[49]

For the most part Robinson seeks mutual correction and complementarity between the two poles of experience. As with Küng, he
acknowledges the need for mutual exploration of religious truth
and mutual critical questioning of one another's traditions in open
dialogue. He accepts that a degree of relativity is attached to his
approach, but refuses to countenance a theology which presses
relativity in religious truth all the way. At this point Robinson
employs a christological argument, leading ultimately to an inclusivism resembling Küng's Christian theology of religions.

In order to retain some criterion among the relativities of religious claims, Robinson stands by the New Testament picture of
Jesus of Nazareth:

Whatever our stretching-points, our sticking-point must be the
reality of this man as embodying, fleshing out, the saving disclosure and act of God.[50]

This is not to say that Robinson affirms the traditional statement of
the Incarnation. Rather he concedes this as essentially mythological. But to call it so does not decide its interpretation. Borrowing
insights from a process theological framework, Robinson's christology is 'from below'. Christ as man defines the reality of God, and
Jesus is the 'human face of God', to quote the title of one of his
earlier books. 'If it helps to say not that God comes down or comes
in but he comes through or even comes out in Jesus, fine.'[51] To
name Jesus as the human face of God is not to be exclusivist;
defining God is not the same as confining him:

It is to dare the conviction, always to be clarified, completed and
corrected in dialogue, that it is this which offers the profoundest
clue to all the rest.[52]

Robinson's view is not an inclusivism which is exclusively determined, which is the impression given by the Catholic theology of religions since Vatican II. The test of Jesus's 'decisiveness' is the ability of the theology which stems from him to deal adequately with questions of suffering, evil, sin, the impersonal and the feminine. Robinson appreciates that this can only be done on the basis of a comparison of religions. After admitting that the vision of Christ is not beyond clarification, completion, and correction, his final verdict is the humble witness *'of those for whom it is true'*:

> Yet I should not be true to my apprehension of the truth if I did not also want to insist that for me the face of God as Father in the cross of Christ and the disclosure of man's destiny 'as in a son' represents the interpretation of the less than personal in experience by the personal in a manner and to a degree that I do not see anywhere else.[53]

The Christ-likeness of God and the provision for clarification, completion and correction summarize this open-ended inclusivism.

In his theory Robinson walks a tight-rope. He is careful not to be too contentious but is not afraid of sometimes sharpening up differences. He sees the need, ultimately, to make a decision between the confessional incompatibilities, but it is a confessional decision which is made *a posteriori* after due consideration of the other eye on truth and the check against the secular experience of the world. He is honest about his own limitations to view the truth as two-eyed, but his inclusivism is open-ended and not exclusively determined. In short, it is a Christian theology of religions which claims not to have pre-judged the issues.

The same question that we raised against the theory of Küng can be asked of Robinson's approach. Both stand mid-way between the full pluralist theology and the inclusivism of the post-Vatican II Catholic approach exemplified by Rahner. Is this 'open inclusivism' a viable approach to either? The former theory states that the God who has many names stands at the centre of the religious universe, and all faiths approximate to truth in relation to it. The latter is firm that the Christian God names the centre, and other faiths approximate to the knowledge of God we have been given in Christ. Is there an either/or here which is theologically more consistent than both/and? There is a sense in which the tension remaining in Robinson's theory is brought to sharp focus in his christology. Holding to Jesus as our 'sticking-point' runs counter to the claim that his 'decisiveness', that which 'offers the profoundest clue to all the rest', can be determined only after comparison with the other focal figures of religion and contributions from the other faiths. This unresolved element will be illustrated further in our chapter on christology and the Christian theology of religions, but it is probably sufficient to jeopardize the final credibility of this whole approach. It is commendable to adjure absolutist categories in an age when 'truth is two-eyed', and to wish to resolve the christological issue 'from below', but it is a moot point how far this christology can stand being 'clarified, completed and corrected' before this version of inclusivism topples. It may be possible to assent to the conclusion that in Christ all things hang together (Col. 1.17), but this must not be pre-judged, even by a christology 'from below', if it is to be acceptable to those who recognize God at work in all the world's faiths. As with Küng, then, Robinson leaves us pondering how far it is possible to engage in a mutual critical dialogue without pre-judging the issue of truth.

We have noted two types of inclusivist theory in the Christian theology of religions. We saw that the first, exemplified by the 'anonymous Christianity' of Rahner, bore many resemblances to the older theology of Luke-Acts, the Fathers, and J. N. Farquhar. This observation itself raised a question: in the light of the growing historical awareness of the last 200 years, is the extension of an old theory a sufficient response to the challenge posed by the new knowledge of the history of religions? My answer has been that the challenge has not been met with judgment or argument which takes sufficiently seriously the questions posed by the new knowledge. The major problem which these theories face is the way in which they pre-judge the issue of religious truth. In an age that values the historical and empirical, to say that one religion contains the fullest expression of religious truth and value, without any recourse to the empirical data of the other religions themselves, is tantamount to an unjustified theological imperialism. In this respect the openness since Vatican II in Catholic theology is only partial and begs many questions. Küng has moved away from his earlier commitment to this kind of inclusivism towards an 'inclusive Christian universalism claiming for Christianity not exclusiveness, but certainly uniqueness'.[54] Along with Robinson, this could be said to exemplify a second type of inclusivism. With this theory the question of criteria in the search for truth becomes the most pressing concern. Both versions of inclusivism pre-judge the issue of truth, though we may commend their nervousness about relativism in religious truth. The new knowledge of the history of religions raises most problems in the area of christology. As long as the claim that Christ represents the fullest expression of the Godhead is maintained without qualification in the light of the new knowledge, then a reformulated inclusivism is the most open option in the theology of religions. But it may be that a Christian theology of religions is possible which remains open to the non-Christian faiths as ways of salvation, without pre-judging the issue of truth, and which gives a positive account of the Christian tradition at the same time. If this is so, then the question the Church Fathers asked, 'Why did Christ come so late', noted by Küng in his earlier work, will receive a more satisfactory answer than an inclusivism which has been updated from its earlier version in Christian history.

4

PLURALISM

Throughout its history, Christian theorizing about the relationship between the Christian and the non-Christian faiths has been ambivalent. The theories of exclusivism and inclusivism can both claim ample pedigree in the Christian tradition, stretching back to the New Testament. It is perhaps inevitable in a historically-minded age, such as our own, that the theologian should first delve into the Christian past in the search for a Christian understanding of our subject sufficient for today. Symptomatically, this is simply a measure of the self-consciousness which characterizes theological writing at the present time. Yet the self-consciousness inherent in this procedure also suggests that the answers forthcoming from the tradition may be inadequate in the face of the new circumstances and needs which initiated the sifting of the tradition in the first place. Historical enquiry makes us aware of both continuities and discontinuities in relation to the past. The question before the church therefore is whether the answers given in the past to the theological issue of Christianity's relationship to the other faiths are sufficient to furnish the church with answers to the problem as it presents itself now. Undoubtedly the exclusivism typified by Barth and Kraemer has dominated discussion of the problem for the greater part of the last fifty years, at least since the publication of Kraemer's *The Christian Message in a Non-Christian World* in 1938. But if the exclusivist account fails to satisfy some fifty years later, this does not mean that any other way forward is necessarily clearer. As Wilfred Cantwell Smith has said:

The fallacy of relentless exclusivism is becoming more obvious than is the right way of reconciling a truly Christian charity and perceptivity with doctrinal adequacy.[1]

The reconciliation I take Cantwell Smith to have in mind here is between God's activity in Christ and his presence working for salvation in the other faiths. Once exclusivism is rejected, the way is opened for a more positive approach to the theological issues of religious pluralism. Catholic theology since Vatican II, under the leadership of Karl Rahner, has proffered its own particular contribution in respect of the move towards a more positive recognition of 'unique grace and religious authenticity everywhere'.[2] Yet we have found reasons why even these moves towards inclusivism were less than adequate for the new situation challenging the church. In this chapter we turn to consider the theories, sometimes termed 'liberal', most closely associated with the names of Ernst Troeltsch, W. E. Hocking and Arnold Toynbee. They provide the background and foundation for some of the recent formulations of a Christian theology of religions, proposed by Paul Tillich, John Hick and Wilfred Cantwell Smith, to name probably the most well known who belong to the same tradition. The pluralism of this chapter refers therefore to a range of other possible options in the reconciliation of a 'truly Christian charity and perceptivity with doctrinal adequacy'. Though its pedigree in Christian history is virtually non-existent before the modern period, there is one early instance of pluralism worthy of mention. In the middle of the fifteenth century Nicholas of Cusa, a Cardinal and member of the Papal Court, wrote his book *De Pace Fidei* (The Peace between Different Forms of Faith). He imagines a conversation in heaven between representatives of the great religions when the divine Logos explains their unity: 'There is only one religion, only one cult of all who are living according to the principles of Reason (the Logos-Reason), which underlies the different rites . . . The cult of the gods everywhere witnesses to Divinity . . . So in the heaven of (Logos) Reason the concord of the religions was established.'[3] At a time when the crusading ethos was still dominant in the church, Nicholas of Cusa anticipated much of a spirit of tolerance more characteristic of the Enlightenment and the present day. It is with this notion of 'tolerance' that we begin our analysis of the pluralist theories in the Christian theology of religions.

Tolerance of another religious position has always been a major hallmark of the Christian liberals. One response to the missionary crisis dawning at the end of the last century was to redefine the missionary task in the light of tolerance. This appeared, for example, in the report of the Layman's Missionary Movement of North America:

> It is clearly not the duty of the Christian missionary to attack other faiths ... The Christian will regard himself as a co-worker with the forces within each religious system which are making for righteousness.[4]

Two forms of tolerance, closely connected but distinguishable, are highlighted in this citation: tolerance as a Christian moral imperative, and as a Christian theological necessity. With moral tolerance Barth and Kraemer would have agreed; they too would not have wished to attack adherents of other faiths by forcing belief on them. But tolerance as a Christian theological necessity was anathema to them. For what is implicit theologically in the invitation to be a 'co-worker for righteousness' is made explicit elsewhere:

> The relation between religions must take increasingly hereafter the form of a common search for truth.[5]

This underlines one essential feature of the theology we might term tolerant pluralism: knowledge of God is partial in all faiths, including the Christian. Religions must acknowledge their need of each other if the full truth about God is to be available to mankind. It also distinguished tolerant pluralism from the inclusivism of the Vatican II Catholic theologians, who view Christianity as the final locus of religious truth.

As a basis for a positive relationship between the faiths tolerance was most passionately defended by Arnold Toynbee. He argues for both kinds of tolerance as a corollary of the belief that God is love. Of theological tolerance he writes:

> I think that it is possible for us, while holding that our own convictions are true and right, to recognize that, in some measure, all the higher religions are also revelations of what is true and right. They also come from God, and each presents some facet of God's truth.[6]

Now it may be possible for Toynbee to defend his conviction that
God has revealed the truth about himself in diverse ways throughout history as a basis for a Christian theology of religions, but as
stated here it lacks proper justification. For example, he has no
answer to the problem of the conflicting truth-claims between
religions. He does not pursue the question whether the different
notions of truth are to be viewed as complementary, or identical, or
whether one is fulfilled in another. The possibility that God's
revelation of himself has been received in history according to
differing cultural contexts is hinted at by Toynbee but not taken
up in the course of argument. For the moment we note that theological tolerance for tolerance's sake usually results in indifference,
the view which counts all faiths (ultimately) the same. Not that
Toynbee would have accepted that as a legitimate judgment of
himself. He was, for instance, against syncretism in religion in
spite of the tendency to come close to this when he says that the
Bahai temple in Chicago 'may be a portent of the future'.[7]

Toynbee's is a historian's point of view. In places there is an
echo of Hegel's progressive philosophy of history whereby the
highest and therefore best religion will automatically evolve to provide the religious foundations for a future world culture:

In peaceful competition, the best of the competing religions will
eventually win the allegiance of the whole human race.[8]

Not only does this appear to contradict his admiration for the
Bahai temple where competition is rejected; but, more seriously,
an automatic evolution of a world religion is by no means a pre-
dictable outcome of history, and many would argue against it even
as a desirable goal. Still, Hegel apart, theological problems remain
with Toynbee. This is probably so because his real concerns were
in the direction of moral tolerance:

The crucial point that I want to make is that we can have conviction without fanaticism, we can have belief and action without
arrogance or self-centredness or pride.[9]

Beyond this Toynbee's real motive for promoting inter-religious
'co-operation' was to preserve the spiritual dimensions of the
emerging 'one world', which were under threat from the forces of

Nationalism and Communism. Respect for the freedom and integrity of other faiths is compulsory for people of all faiths if the struggle to protect the reality of spiritual faith itself is to succeed. In these circumstances the proper decision for Christianity, according to Toynbee, would be to lay aside its claim to absolute supremacy.

It may be that the pressure to work towards one world faith to equip an emergent world community was particularly strong in the minds of the more liberal thinkers in the middle years of this century. W. E. Hocking, for example, was another who attended to the question as a high priority:

> With it, the question is bound to arise whether a world religion is not a necessary accompaniment of world culture, and if so, what sort of religion it must be.[10]

He shares the same desire for tolerance as Toynbee, but his approach to it, designated the 'Way of Reconception', displays a more alert sense of the theological problems involved in working for a world faith. Hocking's theory was built on the theological premise that all religions contain an inalienable core of truth, expressed in diverse ways:

> In proportion as any religion grows in self-understanding through grasping its own essence, it grasps the essence of all religion, and gains in power to interpret its various forms.[11]

The way is paved for a world faith because as each faith strives to reconceive itself in the light of insights and truths which belong to the heart of the other faiths, and are only fully available within them, each faith discovers, not only more adequately and completely its own essence, but also the essence of all religious truth.

For Hocking, then, the essence of all religion is a future reality. Moreover, it is acceptable in so far as it appears to counter the objections which most theories of essence suffer, namely, that they involve a stripping down of a religion to its barest minimum, discarding all but the centre. It is a highly questionable enterprise to reduce a religion by such drastic measures; the concern of a religion is more than talk of mere essence conveys. Nevertheless, the projection into the future of the discovery of the essence of religion does not completely overcome the dilemma. There is still an assumption that at their theological roots the religions share the same essence. In which case the second objection to which theories of essence are prey applies: they fail to take adequate account of the very different apprehensions of God and the world present in the different religions. Of course, on a practical level, the issue ought not to be pre-judged. One of the features of religions is that they are not entities, but are continually changing and developing. It may be that the essence of all religion would unfold if the way of Reconception was attempted, though Hocking himself says, 'It comes to no final stopping place.'[12] Yet the basic question remains: can a Christian theology of religions which deals in categories of essence deal adequately with the different apprehensions of reality which the religions profess?

Further elements of Hocking's theory are revealed when he described how Reconception proceeds. The power of one faith to interpret another is bound to assume that one faith anticipates the meaning of the other, 'opening to them that larger room toward which they trend'.[13] Ultimately Hocking views Christianity as the larger room:

> In its ideal character, Christianity is the 'anticipation of the essence' of all religion, and so contains potentially all that any religion has.[14]

This resembles a fulfilment approach, and one wonders whether Hocking has pre-judged the issue altogether at this point. However, this would be a little unfair, as he makes this statement only after examining some of what he terms 'emerging filaments of faith',[15] which are dominant elements of religion constituting a sort of rudimentary 'natural religion'. These are convictions which arise out of the searching soul of man down the centuries and would come to fruition in an emerging world faith. Christianity is believed to be the faith most theologically commensurate with these demands of the soul. Even so, the sense of a fulfilment approach lingers on with this theory.

The real motive behind Hocking's way of Reconception is the desire for one world faith. Perhaps this is why 'essence' and 'fulfilment' appear somewhat contrived forty years later. Yet Hocking is not without his genuine insights. There is validity in pointing out there must be something in common between religions in order for them to be recognized by the same term itself and be distinguished from other cultural dimensions. If the search for a world faith is not now the major concern in the relations between religions, this does not mean that in the present mood of dialogue some measure of reconception will not be called for if the religions are to advance in mutual understanding. Maurice Wiles, for example, views the development of Buddhistic and Islamic forms of Christian theology as a necessary step in the wider ecumenical vision which is the model for the way forward in dialogue between the faiths:

> May we perhaps look forward in the long run to the emergence of distinctively Buddhistic and Islamic forms of Christian theology? By those terms I envisage forms of Christian theology in which insights central to Buddhism and Islam – and only fully accessible and expressed within those faiths – will have been allowed to mould and modify Christian belief in a way which will illuminate and deepen aspects of belief implied but only imperfectly realized in other forms of Christian theology.[16]

The precedence for such developments is given in Christian history. For example in the encounter with the Hellenistic world, when Christian faith appropriated platonized forms of belief, it did so in ways which were far from syncretistic. By the same token, Wiles believes the development of different forms of Christian belief may point some of the way forward. Given the rider that this should not rule out critical judgments, Hocking may have provided a useful contribution if progress in the relations between the faiths is to be along these lines.

'Tolerance' and 'Reconception' embodied a number of genuine insights. Of particular importance was the realization that religious truth cannot escape cultural relatedness. Now this is true of any claim to truth or knowledge. Its corollary in religious truth is the hypothesis that the diverse forms and patterns of experience and belief, manifest in the religions, represent different 'cultured responses' to the same ultimate divine reality. Christianity in this theory represents only one cultured response to the divine initiative; it cannot claim a monopoly of religious truth. This view, sometimes termed 'relativism', was an integral part of the tolerance exemplified, for instance, by Toynbee:

76

And it would seem unlikely that He would not have given His revelation in different forms, with different facets, and to different degrees, according to the difference in the nature of individual souls and in the nature of the local tradition of civilization. I should say that this view is a corollary of the Christian view of God as being love.[17]

As a theory in the Christian theology of religions this view has a *prima facie* attractiveness; it is the simplest solution to the problem of mankind's religious diversity. But I have already said that in this bare outline form it is insufficient. For example, what is the nature of religious truth, given the initial hypothesis? It is problematic enough to compare religious statements within one variegated tradition. When the comparison extends across cultural boundaries the difficulties are manifestly increased. How are judgments between religions now to be made? Criteria for the task have still to be formulated and lie at the heart of the pluralist theory.

Not least among the problems is the misunderstanding that surrounds the word 'relativism'. The difficulties relate to the number of meanings it has.[18] In one sense 'all is relative'; that is, everything which exists does so in relation to everything else. More philosophically, relativism means that all human apprehensions of truth are necessarily limited, partial, and conditioned by the environment of the subject. There is always a distinction between the knower and the known such that unconditioned knowledge can never be available, by definition, to persons limited by particular environments. If this epistemological principle carries implications for the status of knowledge in all areas of human understanding, how much greater are the implications for theological understanding, when the gap between knower and known is that between the finite and the infinite. In fact religions have recognized this peculiar status of religious knowledge whenever theology has spoken of the divine in terms of images and analogies. In this sense relativism is unavoidable. In the present context, however, relativism is applied in a third sense. It is the belief that there is not one, but a number of spheres of saving contact between God and man. God's revealing and redeeming activity has elicited response in a number of culturally conditioned ways throughout history. Each response is

77

partial, incomplete, unique; but they are related to each other in that they represent different culturally focussed perceptions of the one ultimate divine reality. This is also sometimes termed pluralism, and is the expression preferred in the present work.

The apparent danger of pluralism in the Christian theology of religions is that if all religious traditions are made relative it could undermine concern to distinguish good from bad, the spiritually wholesome and profound from the spiritually poor and moribund religion. It could imply the first steps towards an undifferentiated syncretism and that choice between the traditions would be rendered arbitrary or meaningless. Stated starkly, it could mean that if all faiths are equally true, then all faiths are equally false. For Barth and Kraemer this 'debilitating relativism'[19] was the inevitable outcome of allowing the history of religions any significance at all for the Christian theologian. Heeding those warning bells, any pluralist position which chooses not to side-step but to pass through the history of religions, will need to counter that kind of relativism. I shall first outline the wider context in which the question of relativism first appeared in connection with our problem, and then discuss a number of recent proposals which attempt to embrace the pluralist position in a positive form as the way forward for Christians.

The rise of the so-called historical consciousness, and the search for a historical method appropriate to it, created a crisis in theology which has been the subject of theological debate for most of this century. Increased knowledge of the history of other faiths created an impact which was but part of the impact of the 'fundamental historicizing of all our knowledge and feeling about the mental world'.[20] Ernst Troeltsch was one of the first to deal rigorously with the implications of this for Christianity's claim to absolute validity and truth. At one level the crisis arose because he discerned a 'fundamental conflict between the spirit of critical scepticism generated by the ceaseless flux and manifold contradictions within the sphere of history and the demand of the religious consciousness for certainty, for unity, and for peace'.[21] Yet the crisis was more than a reiteration of Lessing's earlier dictum[22] that the probabilities of history cannot yield the certainty religious faith requires. It points also to a dissonance between a theological interpretation of history and culture which is *a priori* given and one which can be affirmed only on the basis of the historical method. Thirdly, the nature of historical reality as an unbroken, inter-related continuous flow of events, 'a continuous connection of becoming',[23] rules out, Troeltsch believes, Christianity's claim to self-authenticating validity. As A. O. Dyson has put this aspect of the crisis of historicism:

> It is also a clash between that view which takes with fullest seriousness the extraordinary diversity of human history, and one which regards human history as somehow focussing upon, and shaped by, a history of salvation in a certain line of human history.[24]

These three consequences of the historical consciousness raise a major question mark against Christianity's claim to religious truth based on a supernatural account of its origins. Moreover, once the historical method is accepted, then the supremacy of Christianity can only be ascertained after comparing it with the other great faiths.

In his earlier phase Troeltsch thought this could be achieved. As he expressed the task:

> The problem faced by the modern approach to history is not that of making an either/or choice between relativism and absolutism but that of how to combine the two.[25]

He proposed that it was possible to discern within the varieties of religious life norms or criteria of judgment whereby the major faiths could be assessed, evaluated and ranked in some kind of order. Comparison between faiths led Troeltsch to conclude that Christianity alone was unique in its claim to absolute validity:

> Among the great religions, Christianity is in actuality the strongest and most concentrated revelation of personalistic religious apprehension.[26]

Historical science, it should be noted, cannot determine which religious tradition is superior; ultimately it is a matter of personal conviction. Troeltsch recognized this, but the historical method dictated that his subjective judgment be grounded in the objective facts. This was why it was necessary to set about comparing religions. Though all religions make some claim to absolute truth (hence their success as religions), comparison between religions revealed to Troeltsch that Christianity alone was both the least wedded to factors of race or nation and also the highest example of personal spiritual faith. The judgment was tenuous, as Troeltsch demonstrated twenty years later. In this later phase he altered his views on both points. On the one hand he showed how firmly Christianity was linked to European cultural values, and, on the other, that the oriental religions were found to contain within them, in different ways, spiritual and humane values akin to many Christian aspirations. These two observations led Troeltsch to disclaim Christianity as the supreme expression of religious life. It is one manifestation of the divine life in one culture:

> The evidence we have for this remains essentially the same, whatever may be our theory concerning absolute validity – it is the evidence of a profound inner experience. This experience is undoubtedly the criterion of its validity, but, be it noted, only of its validity *for us*. It is God's countenance as revealed to us; it is the way in which, being what we are, we receive, and react to, the revelation of God.[27]

The relativism proposed here does not disenfranchise Christianity of its profound spiritual worth, but views it as one faith among others, 'a purely historical, individual, relative phenomenon, which could, as we actually find it, only have arisen in the territory of the classical cultures, and among Latin and German races'.[28] Furthermore it does not lessen Christianity's hold on religious truth:

> A truth which, in the first instance, is *a truth for us* does not cease, because of this, to be very Truth and Life.[29]

Of course it is possible to maintain that these restrictions on the universal validity of Christian truth do rob Christianity of spiritual profundity. But, for Troeltsch, this conclusion was not requisite.

There is some unease about Troeltsch's discussion at this point. It derives from the intellectual and psychological instinct that something cannot be true *for us* without also being true for all mankind.[30] Is there a logical fallacy here? The difficulty is that Troeltsch has made us aware that religions are total *Weltanschauungen* 'conceptually or symbolically embracing everything: the world, as a whole and in parts, human life, human destiny, good and evil, actuality and potentiality, transcendence and the infinite, truth'.[31] It is not a case of ruling out one religious position in favour of another in the manner that Western logic suggests. Evaluation of religious traditions is more subtle than making that kind of straightforward choice. 'To judge one by the criteria of another is clearly a whit inept.'[32] Religion not only is dependent upon culture for its expression, but also provides a foundation for culture itself. The two are inextricably bound together. Comparison and choice between whole civilizations in this respect is obviously not a logical issue. Once this has been said, the sense of a logical fallacy recedes to the background.

Logic apart, the unease about Troeltsch's position persists. He seems to have arrived at a position symptomatic of the 'wretched historicism' he himself despised. This 'wretched historicism' means a collapse of human values and the abandonment of any criteria, any controlling standard for the interpretation of religious-cultural history. Troeltsch was searching for a theology which would furnish cultural history with a religious foundation. Having abandoned himself to the historical method *in toto*, the 'wretched historicism' could only be overcome after a survey of the cultural history of the whole world, or at least, to begin with, of the West. This was a massive enterprise, of which a theology of religions was only a part, and which Troeltsch's death forestalled. For the moment we note that his solution to the 'wretched historicism' lay not in any human decision but in the being of God himself, 'where alone the ultimate unity and the final objective validity can lie'.[33] A weakness of Troeltsch at this point is that he gives no theological justification for the belief that all faiths derive from the same source and tend towards the same goal. The religions do characterize their inner meaning and essence differently. If they tend towards the same goal, then the differing elements of religious experience within them will require careful alignment and comparison. This point is taken up by later theologians.

The shift in Troeltsch's thought occurred as a result of his researches in sociology and history. It had become clear that any future theology could only bypass the culturally related nature of religious patterns of belief and practice at the cost of an essential insight into the nature of religious knowledge and truth. For those who accept the incursions of historical science into theological method, as the only valid procedure in an age of increased historical consciousness, Troeltsch's work is paradigmatic. Broadly speaking we may assent to his theological method, as one consonant with the 'fundamental historicizing of all our knowledge and feeling about the mental world', in spite of a number of remaining problems with his approach, and in spite of some reservations over the picture of the relationship between religion and culture he painted in his later thought. The further theological justification of his pluralistic outlook we shall consider shortly. The reservations concern a criticism that he tended to link religion with the race rather than culture. There are errors, for instance, in his confining Islam as the religion of the Arab peoples only, forgetting that the majority of Muslims live outside of the Middle East in Russia, Pakistan, Bangladesh, India and Africa. Again, he links Buddhism simply to the tropical countries, ignoring its development through China, Tibet and Japan. And Christianity too he confined narrowly to the Latin and Germanic peoples. With the correction that Buddhism, Christianity, Islam, Hinduism are the best understood as religious cultures which exist across racial and ethnic divides, Troeltsch's work represents the real beginning of the argument for pluralism in the Christian theology of religions.

Once it was admitted that God was at work positively in the history of religions, it became impossible to ignore Troeltsch's pioneering work. One theologian who has attempted to provide further theological justification for Troeltsch's theory is John Hick. He terms his pluralistic scheme a 'Copernican Revolution'. As the sun replaced the earth at the centre of the planetary universe so too God ought to replace Christ and Christianity at the centre of the religious universe:

> And we have to realize that the universe of faiths centres upon *God*, and not upon Christianity or upon any other religion. He is the sun, the originative source of light and life, whom all the religions reflect in their own different ways.[34]

Hick demonstrates how the pluralist solution makes sense historically and theologically. Historically the religions have grown from the axial period of religious experience (Hick cites this phrase from Karl Jaspers *The Origin and Goal of History*, Routledge and Kegan Paul, London 1953) which occurred from about 800 to 200 BC, in geographical isolation from one another. Given those historical facts it was not possible for there to be one revelation to the world, which could be received in one theological form. This burgeoning of religious life could be interpreted as the same divine Spirit finding a response in the human spirit, a process which comes to expression in various cultural forms as the world faiths. The hypothesis proposes that at the level of experience the religions portray a genuine, though different, encounter with the divine, and that the differences between religious beliefs and practices reflect the cultural forms and circumstances which embody the experiences. Discrepancies between the faiths at the level of theological statement can be interpreted more as an occasion for reconciliation in the greater all-encompassing truth of the infinite divine reality than for rivalry. Both aspects of Hick's argument deserve comment.

Whilst it is, on the whole, a true observation, it is important not to stress the point about geographical isolation too far. Religions have been coming into contact (and conflict) with neighbours for much of their history. To single out two instances: neither Hinduism and Buddhism, nor Christianity and Judaism, are explicable without references to each other. Furthermore, religions define themselves not only according to their own intrinsic impulse but also in relation to their environment, which often includes other potentially rival religious claimants. Perhaps it is more true to say that the isolation has been most obvious between East and West, between the mystic and prophetic centres of religious life. None the less, one can defend the Copernican Revolution in so far as it is submitted as a possible Christian theology of religions for today's 'one world'. The foundation of Hick's hypothesis is that religious experience represents a *genuine* encounter with the one ultimate divine reality. Major religions have flourished, providing the roots of, and in turn being moulded by, whole cultural worlds. Attention is given to the subject which goes beyond the realization that religions have struggled against each other in a bid to define themselves. Nor is the 'Copernican Revolution' claiming that religious truth is wholly determined by geography, with the consequence that all expressions of it are equally valid. It is claiming that geography has played a major role in shaping religious truth as it has come down to us diversely through history, and this cannot be ignored in the attempt to give expression to religious truth today.

There is good reason, initially, to say that the major faiths make unique sounds which then contribute to a symphonic whole. This leads to the more theological aspects of the 'Copernican Revolution'.

In his earlier work Hick distinguished three components of the theological problem:

> ... differences in modes of experience of the divine reality; differences of philosophical and theological theory concerning that reality; and differences in the key, or revelatory, experiences that unify a stream of religious experience and thought.[35]

These distinctions represent aspects of the one problem and are not three separate problems. Their usefulness lies in the provision of a clear framework for discussion of the issues. We shall consider each in turn.

The first of the distinctions poses a problem of the identity of the one ultimate divine reality. How is it possible to say that different experiences stem from the same divine reality? Hick's answer is to note, first, that all the major faiths recognize that it is ultimately impossible to confine and circumnavigate the infinite with finite human language. The Ultimate exceeds all our thoughts and speculations. The 'God' whom our minds can comprehend is a human image, inadequate and incomplete, of what is ultimately indefinable. If this is accepted, then the way is opening for us to view the different reports of religious awareness of the divine as complimentary and not as mutually exclusive. This is not merely an assertion that we cannot know absolutely the absolute truth, for that would be a contradiction. Rather, it states that all religions see through a glass darkly, and it is this which makes possible the hypothesis of a new universe of faiths. Now in his earlier work Hick attempted to give further justification for his hypothesis by drawing on the phenomenology of religious experience. The major difficulty arose over the division between the theistic and the non-theistic faiths. Given the very different reports of religious experience across this division, how is the hypothesis to stand? A tentative answer was to point to a certain measure of overlap across this divide. While the differing elements of religious experience tend to be concentrated separately in different forms of religious life, so that the prophetic and the experience of personal encounter with the divine are dominant in the semitic faiths, and mystic and non-personal union with the divine are dominant in the Asiatic faiths, there is nevertheless some minimal degree of common ground. So, for example, Christianity does contain a strand of impersonal experience of God in the mysticism of Meister Eckhart, and Paul Tillich has spoken of the impersonal Ground of Being. On the other hand Hinduism contains within it a major strand which stresses the personal presence of the divine reality; and even early Buddhism, though with some considerable strain, could be made to fit into this picture.

Now part of the problem with this reliance on the phenomeno-logy of religious experience is that it is not possible to make such easy judgments about shared common ground. Ninian Smart, for example, is sceptical about such reliance:

> From a phenomenological point of view it is not possible to base the judgment that all religions point to the same truth upon religious experience.[36]

Even where the experience appears to be similar, for instance in mysticism, there are varying reports of the unitive mystical state which suggests characteristically different experiences. There are certainly some common elements, but the general observation of phenomenology disallows any simple assertion of complementarity. In more recent writing Hick shows himself to be in agreement with these phenomenological conclusions and turns to a more philo-sophical account of religious experience and its interpretation in order to develop his hypothesis further.

The suggestion that the one ultimate divine reality is experienced in different forms according to different cultural environments involves a distinction between 'God as infinite being' and 'God as finitely experienced'. From a phenomenological point of view, this distinction is present in all the major religions. On the one hand 'God' is beyond conceptualizing powers of the human mind, and on the other hand he is related to or worshipped through human perceptions or images, which are sometimes personal, sometimes impersonal. Hick now unfolds further justification for his hypothe-sis by borrowing from one strand of Kant's general epistemology of how human beings experience and interpret in sense-perception, applying it analogously to the awareness of the one ultimate divine reality in the world faiths. Kant distinguished between the noumenal world and the phenomenal world. The former was said to exist independently of human perception and the latter was said to be the world as it appeared to human consciousness. Man's perception of the world, that is, as the phenomenal world of human experience, was said to result from the collaboration between the categorizing conceptual framework of the human mind, and the impact of information from external noumenal reality. The human mind made its own contribution as a sort of filter in the business of interpreting experience. As this is applied analogously to religious awareness, the noumenal world is paralleled with the conception of 'God as infinite being', and the phenomenal world with 'God as humanly experienced'. As Hick has written:

> The varying divine personalities worshipped in their respective religious traditions, and likewise the varying non-personal forms in which God is known in yet other religious traditions, are all alike divine phenomena formed by the impact of God upon the plurality of human consciousness.[37]

It is important to stress that Hick is applying an epistemological model from Kant, who himself did not believe that God could be experienced, even as divine phenomenon. Basing the hypothesis on religious experience as veridical Hick believes that the range of divine phenomena are the divine noumenon as humanly experienced in terms of a variety of images of the one ultimate divine reality.

Hick's use of Kant is very illuminating and provides considerable backing for the hypothesis of the 'Copernican Revolution'. It also clarifies some points of objection raised by his critics. Duncan B. Forrester, for instance, has complained:

> One wonders whether perhaps he has not capitulated to a relativism which is unlikely to be acceptable to committed believers except for Vedantic Hindus.[38]

Hick's position is, however, significantly different from the Hindu view, which counts the worship of a personal God a preliminary stage of religious life, and is transcended in the state of full enlightenment where God is impersonal being. Hick's view is that both the personal and impersonal conceptions of God are human images and valid ways of approaching the one ultimately indescribable divine reality. Another objection to Hick's view, brought by the same critics, is that he destroys particularity in matters of religious experience, and thus robs it of its vital power. There is some force in this objection, especially when we note that Hick has latterly turned to a philosophical justification for his theory. But it is important, also, not to press the objection too far. In defence of Hick we can admit that his intention is not to destroy religious particularity, but to view different types of religious experience as complementary and not mutually exclusive. There is, however, one remaining problem with the hypothesis of the 'Copernican Revolution', which Hick himself acknowledges. It is the question of the relative validity or adequacy of the images of God which are alive in the different traditions. The pluralist hypothesis leaves open the problem of criteria for evaluating the different images of the divine. To that matter we shall return; we consider now Hick's second distinction concerning the differences between religions.

Differences in doctrine and theological statement occur at many levels, and on this scheme reflect differences in the historical and cultural factors bound up in religious belief. Examples could be: the Indian doctrine of reincarnation against the Judaeo-Christian belief of one life in this world; the Indian belief in the cyclical nature of history against the belief that history is the stage for purposeful action of God. Now the foundation of the pluralist hypothesis, that religious experience is veridical, precludes the necessity for agreement at the level of doctrine. It does, however, provide a wider basis for theology than that given by any one tradition, and it is this wider basis which makes constructive dialogue a possibility. What is envisaged is that religions will co-exist in relationship after the pattern established in the Christian ecumenical movement. There will be some common ground; no simple assumption that a single all-embracing statement of truth is ultimately possible or desired; and a process of sharing, listening, and openness to correction and complementarity. Dialogue will also be the setting in which evaluation of the different images of God can take place. Final unity of belief can only be eschatalogical, that is, located in the being of God himself.

The application of the Christian ecumenical model to the relations between religions is in many respects a bold step, even if perhaps inevitable in a pluralistic world. As it has been practised in the Christian world it has been far from satisfactory. Enthusiasm for it waxes and wanes, reflecting, one may suppose, the delicate balance between the necessity to overcome the absurdity of division and the drive to retain identity. But no matter how the model functions in practice, it is not precluded by theological method. Incompatibility between statements in one religious tradition alone is a recognized feature of religious language. Affirmation, for instance, of God's eternity and God's relation to time in Christian theology involves an element of incoherence in the statement of the doctrine. This is not to say that there are no constraints on religious language: paradox cannot be piled on paradox *ad infinitum*. What it does allow is that when the ecumenical model is extended to the Christian theology of religions, apparently contradictory statements may correspond to the complementary truths about the one ineffable God.

Further evidence in support of the plea for a wider ecumenism can be adduced by noting that already there have been moves on both sides of the prophetic-mystic divide towards mutual recognition, and the need for mutual incorporation of some insights from each other's traditions. J. A. T. Robinson, for example, has observed how this has happened in relation to a number of important doctrinal areas (see above p. 65f.). Both the movement towards mutual recognition, and the reverse argument that distortion ensues if each religion presses its own conditioned doctrine too far in isolation, provide support for the ecumenical model of religious truth. Dialogue is a necessity, on this view, for the points of contact and difference between faiths to be clarified. Yet dialogue itself is not without difficulties, and if it proves less than fruitful than anticipated, then, in an important sense, Hick's approach will be called in question. At least its weakness as a viable Christian theology of religions will have been clarified. But we turn now to Hick's third distinction of the one theological problem before considering the process of dialogue in more detail.

The third of Hick's distinctions is the most problematic in the way of religious agreement. For each faith coheres around figures, events and scriptures which, by their revelatory power, have been and continue to be mediators of the holy. And wherever the holy is experienced, it has the character of the 'absolute' which is then easily transferable to, and enshrined in, theological doctrine. 'The absoluteness of the experience is the basis for the absoluteness of the language'.[39] If this happens in a number of separate instances, then the religions easily establish themselves as rival ideological communities, each confessing to an absolute claim on its own discipleship. In Christianity this absoluteness has been enshrined in the doctrine of the Incarnation, whereby God is said to have been utterly and uniquely revealed in Jesus of Nazareth who was fully God and fully man.

Hick realizes that this doctrine is incompatible with his proposed Copernican Revolution. For identification of Jesus as the Christ with God places Jesus, and the events surrounding him (what is sometimes termed 'Christ-event'), at the centre of the religious universe and thus specifies the Christian discipleship of Jesus as the final way to God. For Hick's proposal to work it is necessary to break the ontological identification of Jesus as the Christ with God.

Enormous problems open up at this juncture, for the doctrine of the Incarnation has been held in Christianity to be the cornerstone of the whole faith. However, developments in New Testament and doctrinal studies have shown how it is possible to hold that the doctrine of the Incarnation is a mythological expression. As Hick has written:

> That *God* has been encountered through Jesus is communicated mythologically by saying that he was God the Son incarnate.[40]

No literal meaning can be attached to the doctrine, but it is language which is meant to convey the religion's saving significance of Jesus without the ontological identification with God himself, yet consonant with the 'absolute' character of him as a revelation of God. The doctrine is parasitic upon the fact of the experience of salvation in and through Christ; it functions by evoking the appropriate attitude of faith in the believer, and, in this sense, is said to be true. The issues raised by this radical reinterpretation of the doctrine of the Incarnation are legion and we shall consider them in depth in a later chapter. But we note here that Hick's proposal is not as idiosyncratic as it first appears, for it is in line with many developments in philosophical theology concerning the nature of religious language. For example, we have learned to treat the doctrine of creation less as a literal account of how the universe originated, and more as a way of speaking of the creaturely dependence on the Creator – more existential, less straightforwardly factual. As D. H. Smith has said:

> Where Christians so often go astray is that they take what is definitely mythic and confessional language and treat it literally and historically ... Myth is the vehicle of faith ... if this is recognized it will be seen that Christianity as a religion is not different in kind from other world faiths.[41]

Accepting this account of the function of religious language, it is not difficult to see how it leads to a reinterpretation of the doctrine of the Incarnation, and therefore to a revaluation of Christianity's relationship to the other faiths. It follows from this that Jesus would represent only one focus of the saving work of God, one vehicle of divine disclosure alongside others. In the Christian theology of religions the full-scale pluralism first enunciated by Troeltsch is finally endorsed by Hick.

The pertinent question mark which hovers over all theories of pluralism is how far they succeed in overcoming the sense of 'debilitating relativism' which is their apparent danger. We have noted that Troeltsch's solution was to name God as the final arbiter in matters of truth, thus proposing an eschatological solution to the 'debilitating relativism' which he termed 'wretched historicism'. This left some theological problems. He hinted at a pattern of ecumenism as the best characterization of religious truth in the relations between faiths, and, therefore, as the best way of dealing with the remaining difficulties. Hick presses the ecumenical model, supplying some theological justification for it, in order to counter the incipient charge of 'debilitating relativism'. It involves an optimistic confidence in the processes of discursive dialogue to render what appear contradictory differences as complementary truths. How warranted is this confidence in inter-religious dialogue?

Whilst it has become a commonplace suggestion as the way forward in the relations between the world faiths, the notion of dialogue is an ambiguous one, and therefore potentially confusing.

The word itself conceals a variety of presuppositions and attitudes, which can result in a lack of clarity about the aims and direction of dialogue proper. E. J. Sharpe has noted four distinct types of dialogue.[42] First, there is the endeavour to appreciate the other *person* of faith who professes an allegiance different from one's own (human dialogue). Second, there is the desire to explore the intuitive recognition of a shared experience of the divine (interior dialogue). Third, there is the search for ways in which the truth claims of different faiths may be viewed as complementary and not conflicting (discursive dialogue). Fourth, there is the need to collaborate in working towards solving practical problems in the building up of world community (secular dialogue). The dialogue which the ecumenical model of religious truth presupposes is mainly the third type, but it will involve the first and second type also. Some progress has been made towards this view, for example, in the WCC's proposals about dialogue:

> The aim of dialogue is not reduction of living faiths and ideologies to a lowest common denominator, not only a comparison and discussion of symbols and concepts, but the enabling of a true encounter between those spiritual insights and experiences which are only found at the deepest levels of human life.[43]

We may applaud the desire to go beyond the mere exchange of differences after the manner of comparative theology, and certainly draw attention to the problem about reducing living faiths to a common core statement, but there remains a sense in which the aims of the dialogue in this statement are still not entirely clear in the 'enabling of a true encounter . . . at the deepest levels of human life'. Again, these will involve at least three of Sharpe's categories. About the need to clarify the aims of dialogue Sharpe has uttered a word of warning:

> It is, however, fair to ask, Progress towards what? Unity, certainly, or at least improved communication in that intermediate stage between manifest disunity and future unity into which many feel that we have now entered. In such cases it is by no means clear whether the unity envisaged is organizational, federal, or 'spiritual'.[44]

These words are fair comment. They echo a warning rather than foreclose the processes of dialogue as such. Presumably we can heed the message about the need for clarification of aims without abandoning dialogue altogether. At any rate, there is bound to be some uncertainty and risk attached to dialogue as part of the journey in faith that one faith's deepest insights may be complemented by another's. The balance between respect for one another's beliefs and the openness to changing one's mind, or learning from another tradition, is precarious and will necessarily embrace risk. We have said that the aim of dialogue in the pluralist Christian theology of religions is discursive and not simply confessional. But new discoveries of 'truth', hoped for in the dialogue, will need to be genuine discoveries if the ecumenical model is to be vindicated. Otherwise the tentativeness which surrounds it will not be dispelled, and it will only be judged wrong-headed. In this connection we can recall that dialogue sometimes does fail,[45] indicating that there is still much work to be done in this connection before everyone is convinced of its usefulness or its ability to solve the remaining problems. Nevertheless, some grounds do exist for assuming the ultimate divine reality to be the same reality glimpsed differently in different cultures. But where there is no agreement on this, it is necessary to lay bare as clearly and honestly as possible the concepts, presuppositions and terms of the dialogue if it is to vindicate the original assumption.

There is, then, much work to do in the dialogue between faiths. Seeking new dimensions of 'truth' is a hazardous, if also an exciting venture. One way in which the terms of the dialogue can be made clearer is to set it against the secular interpretations of experience and the critique of religious belief which these involve. For religious faith, if it is to be credible in the modern world, must seek to answer the secular critique of religion while simultaneously demonstrating how it may provide secular culture with a religious foundation. In this respect we fully endorse Hans Küng's suggestion that Christianity in the dialogue between faiths should perform a role of 'critical catalyst'. Christianity, more than any other, believes Küng, is the one faith which has undergone profound changes as a result of the impact of secularization and its accompanying empiricist philosophy and science. The effect of the natural and the human sciences has been shattering on many of the traditional beliefs and values of religious faith. In response to these forces

Christian theologians have been producing ideas, aimed at modifying Christian belief in the light of the new knowledge, in systematic fashion throughout the modern era. As a result Christianity, it could be claimed, has become the most self-conscious faith of all the faiths. In the dialogue this is the Christian gift to the other faiths as they are required more and more to come to terms with the empiricizing and secularizing forces of the modern world. As Küng has put it:

> Christianity therefore should perform its service among the world religions in a dialectical unity of recognition and rejection, as critical catalyst and crystallization point of their religious, moral, meditative, ascetic, aesthetic values.[46]

The gain, however, would not be all one way. Christianity could benefit from the insights of the other faiths in the dialogue. Küng himself suggests that Christians might learn simplicity in dogmatics from Islam with its strong insistence on the one God, or from the Asian faiths in their desire to remove ultimately any anthropomorphic image attached to God, or from the profoundly humanizing Chinese philosophy which may help Christians to correct an over-emphasis on concern with life after death. Other examples, not mentioned by Küng, where the Christian might learn from his other religious neighbours, could be how to handle more sensitively the truth of myths, which Hindu thinking has long been accustomed to; or how to come to terms with 'agreeing to differ', which again has been worked out with sophistication by some Eastern traditions. In all of this it is important to stress that the theoretical presupposition of pluralism in the Christian theology of religions involves dialogue in a common quest for truth where real differences are allowed to be voiced, and the whole is set against the practical and theoretical challenge of the secular world. How to speak of the work of God in and through all the world faiths will depend therefore on a long period of interpenetration and dialogue on many levels. One of the contemporary problems for the Christian theologian is how to conceptualize the activity of God in history. Speaking on this problem A. O. Dyson has written:

> If this can be done at all, I take the view that it will not be achieved simply on the basis of a conjunction of history and

theology, but only and also on the basis of a many-sided view of the situation of man in the world, a theme to which natural science and other human sciences also have a right to contribute.[47]

We should not expect any less, it seems to me, in the dialogue proposed by pluralism if the ecumenical model of truth is to become more than a theoretical assumption.

At times the impression is given that the material presented by the history of religions is so diverse that it seems impossible to bring any sense of order and understanding to bear on it, once the pluralist theoretical assumption is granted. Hick proposed a shift from viewing the religious truth claims as conflicting to complementary; I added the rider that this is subject to confirmation as dialogue unfolds. For some, however, this may still remain insufficient. Powers and criteria for discriminating between good and bad religion, for discerning distortion or exaggeration, may be absent. The criticism is valid, but should not be pressed too far. Such criteria are not given from outside the various traditions. If they exist, they must lie within the depths of the faiths themselves. This is what I have contended in saying that they can only emerge during the course of dialogue. But are there other ways in which the bewilderment, precipitated by the potentially infinite adaptations of religious life, may be overcome in a pluralist Christian theology of religions? We turn now to the theory of Paul Tillich, who proposes a different perspective from that of Hick.

The starting-point of Tillich's theory is the experience of the Holy in the religions. The Holy, he says, whenever it is experienced, proceeds from a sacramental basis which is then developed in the direction of either the prophetic or mystic type of religious expression. In his final lecture before his death Tillich describes the unity of these three elements of religion as the 'Religion of the Concrete Spirit'. This accords, he believes, with the inner aim or *telos* of the history of religions:

> We can see the whole history of religions in this sense as a fight for the Religion of the Concrete Spirit, a fight of God against religion within religion. And this phrase, the fight of God within religion against religion, could become the key for understand-

94

ing the otherwise extremely chaotic, or at least seemingly chaotic, history of religions.[48]

The fight of God within religion against religion refers to the struggle against the abuse and manipulation of the sacramental basis of religion, against those who limit the experience of the divine to any particular manifestation of it. The struggle takes two forms, the prophetic and the mystic. In Christianity the cross represents the denial that the Holy can be contained and manipulated. Even he who manifests God negates himself for the sake of the God who is manifest in him. However, Christianity as such cannot be identified with the Religion of the Concrete Spirit. No guarantees can be supplied for its manifestation. But Tillich, as a Protestant theologian, confesses that he has discovered no higher expression of the Religion of the Concrete Spirit than in Paul's doctrine of the Spirit.[49] In this sense Christianity contains within it the highest potential for a religion that has universal significance.

Tillich's views outlined here represent a development of his earlier work *Christianity and the Encounter of the World Religions.* At this stage the criterion which he used to judge all religions was not the drive towards the Religion of the Concrete Spirit, but the specification of Jesus as the Christ. Tillich was concerned to find a middle way between Barth's exclusivism and Troeltsch's relativism. Whilst rejecting exclusivism, he nevertheless wished to retain the element in Barth which stressed that biblical religion is often portrayed as a struggle against religion, that is, against the manipulation of the God who is above all Gods. The cross of Christ was central as a symbolic representation of the God who refused to be tied down to any particular manifestation of himself:

> What is particular in him is that he crucified the particular in himself for the sake of the universal . . . With this image, particular yet free from particularity, religious yet free from religion, the criteria are given under which Christianity must judge itself and, by judging itself, judge also the other religions and the quasi-religions.[50]

In his later essay Tillich developed his dynamic-typological approach to the point where the history of religions was not pre-judged by the cross, but was regarded as a process, the inner aim of which pointed towards the cross. The cross could then function symbolically to unite retrospectively, as it were, the two major types of religious experiences. Tillich would have agreed with J. A. T. Robinson that Jesus as the Christ offers the 'profoundest clue to all the rest', but his approach via the history of religions proper precluded him from accepting that in any exclusively determined way.

The theology of the later essay of Tillich therefore bears some similarity to the Troeltsch/Hick position; both proceed on the basis of religious experience. However, Tillich's approach differs in two ways. First, it attempts to discern within the varied expression of religious life throughout history an inner aim or *telos*. Second, it leaves open the possibility that there may be a central event in the history of religions which has universal significance even for a historically conscious world. For those who hold that the ecumenical relations between different Christian groups are not very illuminating for the relations between different religions, then Tillich's theory will be more fruitful. The 'relativizing' consequences of Troeltsch are overcome by postulating the intrinsic aim of all religious existence as the Religion of the Concrete Spirit.

Tillich is most vulnerable at the crucial point. One criticism is that the 'Religion of the Concrete Spirit' is too abstract a concept. It is extremely difficult to specify the goal of the religions so that the very discrepancies and disagreements form anything which may be said to be a pattern. Of course, the foundation for any pattern is the experience of the Holy, and Tillich, along with Robinson and Hick here, relies on the observation that all religions contain, explicitly or implicitly, personal and impersonal apprehensions of the Holy:

> Such observations confirm the assumption that none of the various elements which constitute the meaning of the holy are ever completely lacking in any genuine experience of the holy, and, therefore, in any religion.[51]

Again, the solution turns on the conclusions of a sensitive phenomenology of religious experience. It is possible to discern something of a pattern within the rough and tumble of the history of religions, one which drives towards a balance between the communal and individual, the prophetic and mystic, the transcendent and immanent, even towards a recognition of incarnation.as a high point in religious development. The final goal of all religion is stated by R. C. Zaehner as follows:

> All are striving towards the realization of the catholic idea (which is also the authentic doctrine of the Catholic Church), and which in Hinduism was long ago proclaimed on a cosmic scale in the Bhagavad-Gita: for what was revealed to Arjuna in Krishna's stupendous theophany was the coherence of all things in the divine centre – the transfigured body of the lord, whether you call the lord Krishna, Christ, or Buddha . . .[52]

The coherence of all things in the divine centre, a diversity in unity, has strong affinities with Tillich's Religion of the Concrete Spirit as the unity of the three elements of religion, the sacramental, prophetic and mystic. If Tillich is to answer the criticism that his central concept is too abstract and is imposed on the diversity of religious history without careful justification in the phenomenology of religion, then he would need to appeal to the kind of judgments made, for example, by Zaehner. I have cited one instance where this is possible in order to demonstrate that he can enlist some support. We need to remember, however, that Tillich suggested his theory as a 'tentative scheme', and offered it in order to induce others to develop their own theories. But Tillich's initial dissatisfaction with his own scheme should not detract others from building on the genius and insight it contains.

Some form of pluralism in the Christian theology of religions is inevitable, I have said, if historical studies are treated seriously. For many reasons, however, a clear formulation of the pluralist position is not easily forthcoming. The main problem concerns the 'debilitating relativism' which it seems, at least potentially, to espouse. I have outlined two recent theories which claim to have solved this aspect of the problem. Are there any other theories which propose a pluralism without the potentially adverse effects of relativism? The views submitted so far appear not to emphasize the doctrine of Christ's Incarnation and the special character of Christian truth and the knowledge of God that comes through Jesus Christ. But from the same Christian theological standpoint it has been argued that Christ gives permission, as it were, for pluralism to be viewed as a creative breakthrough for Christian theology itself. Far from making a theological virtue out of historical necessity, it is precisely what is required by Christian faith. So J. B. Cobb writes:

> To be a pluralist is not to be neutral with respect to all values. Further, the high appraisal of pluralism does not spring rootless from nowhere . . . For the Christian it can arise only through a deepening of the understanding of Christ.[53]

For Cobb the deepening of the understanding of Christ is achieved when Christ ceases to be identified as an object and instead is identified in the *processes* of creative transformation as they occur in a number of current theological movements. Examples in liberation theology lie close to hand:

> To see Christ in the movements of social, political, economic, ethnic, national, and sexual liberation of our time is to recognise him in the process of creative transformation of basic understanding and of the theology in which that is expressed.[54]

To move from Christian theology to the study of the history of religions is one act of creative transformation. When Christ names the power which enables this to happen, then theology is liberated to embrace pluralism without relativism. Cobb's argument is from within Christian boundaries. It leaves open the question of how far other traditions can appropriate pluralism on their own terms. He quotes a Buddhist scholar, Masao Abe, who has submitted Buddhism for the spiritual foundation of the approaching 'one world'. Because Buddhism is a 'positionless position', it allows all positions relative recognition and truth. This leaves, Cobb realizes, a new pluralism of principles: Christ as creative transformation and the 'positionless position'. The answer to this question, Cobb concludes, we are not yet ready to give.

The virtue of Cobb's contribution is that he combines fidelity to Christ with unqualified openness to other faiths. Elsewhere he says that 'Christ is the way that excludes no ways' (p. 22). It appears at times to represent another version of the Catholic Logos theory. We can recall the Logos was the rational creative principle which ordered the universe and was manifest in human form at the Incarnation. The consequence in Christian theology was that

Christ became the Way completing other ways. Some short-comings of this view were noted in the chapter on inclusivism, the main one being that inclusivism still pre-judged the issue of superiority of 'way'. If Cobb's is another version of the Logos theory, then it is questionable whether he will ever overcome the duality of principles he posits. This he himself partially admits.

Cobb's views have received little attention from British and Continental commentators in our subject. This could be partially due to the abstract nature of his theory. Talk of 'Christ as the principle of creative transformation' is far removed from incarnational talk of him as the person of creative transformation. However, Cobb's work does deserve more attention than it has received to date.

Finally, we turn to consider the work of Wilfred Cantwell Smith, whose contribution to the pluralist theory has attracted considerable attention in recent years. His background as a historian of religion is betrayed in the following quotation:

> The study of comparative religion is the process, now begun, where we human beings learn, through critical analysis, empirical enquiry, and collaborative discourse, to conceptualize a world in which some of us are Christians ... Muslims ... Hindus ... Jews ... sceptics; and where all of us are, and recognize each other as being, rational men and women.[55]

This is the academic task before the student of comparative religion who is aware that as a matter of fact 'we have all along been participants in the world history of religion',[56] though we have only recently come to see that that participation has been diverse and segregated. The academic task arises because there is no other way of conceptualizing a world than through the traditions which are now before us, traditions which include the sceptical rational as well as the religious. Equally there is no 'external' stance from which to judge reality: it is the relativity of 'ideologies' which creates the academic task anew. This understanding of the study of comparative religion forms the background to Cantwell Smith's position in the Christian theology of religions.

A watershed was reached in the Christian conceptualizing of other men's faiths with the publication of Cantwell Smith's *The Meaning and End of Religion* (Macmillan, New York 1962; SPCK,

London 1978). The radicalism proposed in that book was a total shift in the way Christian theologians had hitherto formulated the problem. Cantwell Smith challenges the commonly accepted notions of 'religion' and 'religions' as the appropriate way to conceptualize the diverse religious life of history. 'Religions' as rival ideological communities reflect, he believes, a late stage in the development of the Western history of ideas, produced at the Enlightenment and exported to the rest of the world. A process of reification began in this period which distorted man's religious disposition to the world and God, substituting an objective or external understanding of religious belief and practice for something which was essentially humane, that is, in an important sense, understood only from within. Religion is not a static 'something' which can be checked from outside for its truth content or meaning; rather, it is a process which enables a true relationship with the world and God, it confers meaning. The Enlightenment view, says Cantwell Smith, led to the intractible problem of 'conflicting truth-claims between religions', a notion which was wrongly estimated because it had been wrongly conceived in the first place. Moreover, it had the effect of making the Western rational tradition the final standard in matters of religious truth, and emphasized an overly intellectual approach to the problems of religious pluralism.

As a historian, Cantwell Smith recognizes that religious communities have evolved largely in isolation from one another, but he is reluctant to rest complacently in a form of relativism which refuses to relate the distinct communities. To replace the distorting inherited terminology Cantwell Smith proposes two alternative concepts: 'personal faith' and 'cumulative traditions'. The former connotes the individual's sense of relationship to the divine, the dispositional attitude towards a number of relations:

> Faith is an orientation of the personality, to oneself, to one's neighbour, to the universe; a total response; a way of seeing the world and of handling it; a capacity to live at more than a mundane level; to see, to feel, to act in terms of, a transcendent dimension.[57]

It is a 'global human quality'.[58] On the other hand, the 'cumulative traditions' represent the cultural frameworks within which the faith of men and women has been nurtured, and corresponds to the ever-changing face of religion:

> It is a device by which the human mind may rewardingly and without distortion introduce intelligibility into the vast flux of human history or any given part of it.[59]

The all-important area in the relations between religions is 'personal faith', which is the creative factor over the 'cumulative traditions'. It is also the uniting factor between people of different traditions because it is the real locus of religious truth. The one 'global human quality' is manifest in diverse forms.

We may aver that Cantwell Smith has performed a useful service in his dismantling of the terms in which the problem of conflicting truth-claims between religions was conceived. Theologians are beginning to talk of religion less as an abstract concept, and more as a way of 'seeing' the universe and its relation to the divine. However, the predominant criticism of Cantwell Smith has been directed at his isolation of 'faith' as the central concept in the search for a Christian theology of religions. Is it possible to drive a wedge through the complex reality we call 'religion' and separate a person's 'faith' from the 'cumulative tradition' which has formed him or her? If Cantwell Smith has set aside the important part played by the form of the religious tradition in order to develop a pluralist theory around the notion of 'faith', may he have ignored an essential element in the problem?

In his later book, *Towards a World Theology*, Cantwell Smith has developed his theories further. That God has been at work in diverse ways in the different religious communities of world history, that God 'saves' through the various forms or patterns of religious tradition, and that 'faith' enables a person to participate in the life of God which is so mediated through a tradition, can be defended as a matter of historical fact *and* of Christian theological knowledge. By 'saved' here Cantwell Smith means that which has enabled a truly moral life, that which has released the drive towards living with more than a mundane reference colouring one's goals and aspirations, that which has kept the forces of despair and meaninglessness at bay. All of this, he believes, can be demonstrated historically, as a matter of fact, through one's friendships with people of other faiths. Theologically, he believes, we know that God 'saves' because of what we know through our knowledge of him in Christ. God, so Christian faith tells us, reaches out to all men everywhere in mercy and love. The difference today is that we can now know how he has been doing this in other ways of which we had hitherto been ignorant:

> Those of us who have heard of these and know something of them must affirm with joy and triumph, and a sense of *Christian* delight, that the fact that God saves through those forms of faith too corroborates our Christian vision of God as active in history, redemptive, reaching out to all men to love and to embrace them. If it had turned out God does not care about other men and women, or was stumped and had thought up no way to save them, then that would have proven our Christian understanding of God to be wrong.[60]

Does this mean that Cantwell Smith proposes the belief that all faiths are equally 'true' or adequate, or the same? Here we must refer back to his insistence that religions must not be viewed too externally. But viewed from the 'inside', from the standpoint of persons of different traditions forming one community, the ultimate aim of inter-religious relations is given in the quotation on p. 99 above. In this respect the notion of a ' "Christian" Theology of Comparative Religion' gives way for Cantwell Smith to 'A Theology of Comparative Religion for those among us who are Christians'.

Cantwell Smith is masterly in gathering a wealth of historical material to support his theory, and he goes a long way to explain more clearly the distinction between 'faith' and 'cumulative traditions'. But he does not profess to have solved all the theological problems associated with his scheme. Perhaps the major remaining problem can best be expressed in relation to his notion of 'truth' in religion. Cantwell Smith is at pains to emphasize that religious truth cannot be truth in the abstract; it becomes true in a person's living faithfully according to the light which has been given to him, 'in the sense of enabling those who looked at life and the universe through their patterns to perceive smaller or larger, less important or more important, areas of reality, to formulate and to ponder less or more significant issues, to act less or more truly, less or more truly to be'.[61] We shall return to this way of viewing religious truth in our final chapter, when we shall consider further the persistent problem of 'conflicting truth-claims'. We note now one other point concerning Cantwell Smith's theory. That is, he nowhere considers in detail the christological aspects of the subject. In a brief reference he describes 'revelation' as something which comes through persons and is not given in propositions. He would abandon phrases like 'God was revealed in Jesus Christ', but prefer to speak of God's revelation of himself as this has been glimpsed by persons enabled by faith. Nevertheless, his intention is that the Christian way is now to be seen as one way among a series of ways to life with God. Like Hick, he substitutes God for Christ at the centre:

> This much, however, is perhaps worth saying: that my proposal is unabashedly theocentric, and among its many faults, this at least is a virtue.[62]

The christological issue we shall consider in the next chapter, and seek ways in which the doctrine of the Incarnation can be interpreted so that it does not pre-judge the issue of truth in religion, and hence fill a gap in Cantwell Smith's general position.

Cantwell Smith's proposed shift in emphasis away from 'religion' and 'religions' enables a new experiment in the Christian theology of religions to proceed. (I continue to use the phrase 'Christian theology of religions' whilst disavowing any sense that this means the conceptualizing of the faith of other men and women from within a tightly bounded framework, which imposes a pre-judgment of the issue of the truth of other faith-commitments.) It is but the beginning of a new stage in the history of Christian theology:

> To live in a world of mystery variously symbolized in various ways, and for certain groups of us truly symbolized in such-and-such a way, is a possible vision for the next stage in the religious history of the world; but let us admit that it would constitute a new stage. The conceptualizations to go with the new insights have yet to be hammered out; and how effective they will prove has yet to be tested.[63]

The new vision will not seek to ignore the facts of religious differences in belief and culture, but equally it will be inspired in the confidence that it is God who claims us, not we him, and he is inviting us to closer approximations of his truth for the coming 'one world' community.

To conclude the present chapter with that kind of clarion call would not be totally misplaced. Problems which arose in the comparable encounter of Christianity with philosophy, science and history were hardly solved overnight. There is no reason to suppose that the present encounter of Christianity with other faiths should be any different. Some theologians are at last beginning to wrestle seriously with the issues involved, but they are still peripheral on the agenda of many. I have said the problems of a Christian theology of religions first truly arose as part of the problem of Christianity's involvement with historical studies. It is, however, legitimate to view it as a subject in its own right. This is possible because the faiths are related around a common purpose, the explanation of 'a world of mystery variously symbolized in various ways'. To say this is to pin-point the central struggle for Christian theology: is the encounter with other faiths to be interpreted as a threat or a promise? The answer of the theory I have termed pluralism is unashamedly the latter. But a long period of interpenetration between Christian theology and the material of the history of religions is necessary before the fears contained in the former response can be dispelled.

But the new vision does not lie wholly in the future. Some progress is being made:

> We believe now that the Ultimate Reality upon which the faith of all believers is focused in every religion is the same, though interpretations of his essential nature are still at variance.[64]

Given this initial assumption, the problem of the Christian theology of religions then becomes one of dealing with the variance. An easy syncretism is ruled out. The way forward is suggested in a theory which holds together the different types of religious experience in a creative tension. Of major importance has been the concern throughout to specify the criteria by which the ensuing pattern avoids the debilitating consequences of relativism. The following have been considered: 1. an ecumenical model of truth; 2. the drive towards the Religion of the Concrete Spirit; 3. Christ as the principle of the process of creative transformation;

4. the personal faith of men and women. None is free from attendant difficulties. But all are confident a prolonged period of dialogue on many levels will show that the difficulties are not insurmountable.

5

INCARNATION AND THE CHRISTIAN
THEOLOGY OF RELIGIONS

When Augustine ended his spiritual quest in the Christian faith, having taken up and discarded various religious options on his journey, he said that his conviction was the consequence of hearing the message of the Incarnation of Christ. Only in Christianity did he hear that 'the Word became flesh and dwelt among us'. Now, throughout most of Christian history this doctrine has been held to be the essence of the Christian faith. Certainly it has been couched in a variety of linguistic forms: in terms of the activity of the Logos of God, as in the famous words of the Johannine text; combining two natures in one person, as the Council of Chalcedon defined it, using the classical language of late antiquity; in terms of the descent of the Son of God to earth, as in the creeds; in a more recent expression from a modern theologian, Brian Hebblethwaite: 'The human life lived and the death died have been held to *be* the human life and death of God himself in one of the modes of his own eternal being.'[1] Yet no matter what form of words may have been used, the central meaning of the belief has been thought to be constant. Augustine has been judged to have been correct in singling out the Incarnation as the distinctive core of Christian belief, and in drawing the conclusion that this is where Christianity claims finality *vis-à-vis* other faiths. It would seem, therefore, that in the doctrine of the uniqueness of Christ Christianity has been furnished with a criterion which renders the theological evaluation of the relationship between Christianity and the other faiths a relatively straightforward matter. However, there are two problems associated with this initial estimate of the task.

First, the doctrine of the Incarnation has been subject to search-ing criticism in recent years, and there are a number of theologians who do not now assent to this interpretation of the figure of Jesus and his impact on the world. They speak rather of God's action 'in' and 'through' the person of Jesus, or of Jesus as the agent of God's will and purposes for the salvation of the world. Clearly these newer interpretations open up other possibilities in estimat-ing Christianity's relation to other faiths, most notably the theory of pluralism. Second, the growing positive evaluation of the other faiths as authentic ways of salvation places a strain on the unique-ness of Christ, and calls for some modification of the traditional doctrine. This is not to say that the recognition of God's saving presence in the other faiths ought to determine the doctrine of the Incarnation, but that certain ways of spelling out its meaning in relation to other faiths require modification. Most notably in this regard there has been a shift from exclusivism to inclusivism. The upshot of these two factors is that the relationship between christology and the Christian theology of religions is more complex than was once thought.

The purpose of this chapter, therefore, is to consider christology in two respects; by analysing the interpretation of the Incarnation as a matter of internal debate in Christian theology; and by examin-ing the relations between the three theologies of religions I have described and the various doctrines of Christ which they embody. The complexity arises here because each general theoretical type harbours a number of distinct, but related, positions, so that the same understanding of Christ may be integrated in different ways across the typological boundaries. The belief that Christ is the unique focus of God's revelation in history is not the sole preroga-tive of the exclusivists; it also finds a place in some inclusivist theories. And the belief that Christ is God's agent for salvation is found in both pluralist and some of the inclusivist theories. We begin by reviewing the place and role of the Incarnation, inter-preted in its traditional sense, in the exclusivist and inclusivist theories. The discussion then broadens out into more general considerations of the debate over this traditional interpretation. Finally we examine the new christologies and their place in the inclusivist and pluralist theories.

The Christian faith's dependence on the uniqueness of Christ has often been called 'the scandal of particularity', and it is possible to elevate this particularity to the extent that it excludes or denies all confessions of the knowledge of God other than that deriving from the event of Jesus Christ. This was effectively the position of Karl Barth, and it is still upheld by those who share his general theological outlook. The second half-volume of Barth's *Church Dogmatics* begins with the following words, which make clear his fundamental starting-point as a Christian theologian in the tradition of the Protestant Reformation:

> According to the Holy Scripture God's revelation takes place in the fact that God's Word became a man and that this man has become God's Word. The Incarnation of the eternal Word, Jesus Christ, is God's revelation.[2]

The implications of this fierce particularism for a Christian theology of religions are spelt out in a later passage:

> It is because we remember and apply the christological doctrine of the *assumptio carnis* that we speak of revelation as the abolition of religion.[3]

Barth, of course, understood religion to mean man's misguided and sinful attempt to reach God by his own unaided efforts, and Christianity was as much subject to this judgment as were the other faiths. True religion, he believed, sprang from obedience to God's revelation, which, in this citation, is equated with the Incarnation. But, as we noted above (see Chapter 2), the major problem with exclusivism is that it refuses to take serious cognizance of the effects of critical historical research into Christian origins and history. To that analysis we can add two illustrations of Barth's refusal to grapple with the historical issues, both of which show his weakness from a christological perspective.

First, it is now undeniable fact that the New Testament contains a number of different christologies. The extent to which these derive directly from the person of Jesus is extremely difficult to discern precisely. At any rate, the variety itself suggests that the christologies are the result, in part at least, of the 'interpreting mind' of the New Testament writers. But even more damaging to Barth's outlook than this is that the doctrine of the Incarnation, as he understood it, is not something which is itself presented in scripture. Even the Fourth Gospel, which is often thought to come nearest to it, stops short of what was later characterized as Christian orthodoxy. This means that Barth's dependence on scripture, as stated above, is not as direct and precise as he himself thought. Of course it may be that Incarnation is a true and proper development of what is presented in Holy Scripture, and many have argued precisely that. But Barth would not have countenanced such a precedure; it was arguments precisely of that kind that he thought did not belong in Christian theology.

The second illustration of Barth's lack of interest in the historical questions is his refusal to attach any importance to the 'quest for the historical Jesus' issue. In his short account of the life and thought of Barth, John Bowden notes that in a paper entitled 'Testimony to Jesus Christ', which Barth had been asked to write for a French journal, 'the three pages that he writes are entirely in metaphorical language'.[4] One wonders if it is at all excusable to be so uninterested in the historical search for the 'Jesus of history', especially as the doctrine of the Incarnation has always assumed some foundation in the historical figure. Barth's christology itself is all of a piece with his unhistorical approach and is derived analytically from his doctrine of the Trinity. This means that the Incarnation is pure paradox without any support from historical fact. But as Norman Pittenger has said, this may have the effect of denying the genuine humanity of Jesus:

> if we attempt to confine Incarnation to that individual in his supposed discreteness, we shall find ourselves in the end in a position where we are in effect denying his genuine humanity and thus making of the Incarnation a docetic exception to human conditions, circumstances, and situations.[5]

Barth and his successors would not, of course, accept that indictment, for such an accusation derives from historical judgment. But the question can only be posed again: is not Jesus, and therefore the doctrine of the Incarnation, made more obscure by this short-circuiting of the historical issues?

If the 'scandal of particularity' has been so magnified in Barth's theology as to be unrealistically scandalous, this is not necessarily the direct implication of the doctrine of the Incarnation itself. Other features in Barth's theology have combined with it to

produce exclusivism. The other theory which holds on to the traditional belief in the absoluteness of Christ but embodies it within a
different framework is the inclusivism of many of the Vatican II
theologians. Here the doctrine of the Incarnation is combined with
the principle that God desires the salvation of all people. The new
dispensation of Christ does not abolish the genuine encounter with
God reflected in the ancient faiths of the world, but completes or
fulfils it. Christ, who alone brings salvation, has been at work
unrecognized and un-named at the heart of the non-Christian
faiths. In this account, therefore, some attempt is made to deal
with the historical fact that the major part of mankind has not
known Christ. But it is interesting to note how the increasing impact of historical consciousness, and the concomitant
pressure to make clear the humanity of Jesus, leads to a significant shift in the attempt to solve the christological problem. Karl
Rahner, for example, proceeds 'from below', that is, by acknow-
ledging the full humanity of Christ, before asking in what sense he
can be said to be divine. In this he therefore differs from Karl
Barth, because he is at least prepared to offer some explanation of
how the paradox of the Incarnation can be understood. As Rahner
has said:

> If human nature is conceived as an active transcendence towards
> the absolute being of God, a transcendence that is open and must
> be personally realized, then the Incarnation can be regarded
> as the (free, gratuitous, unique) supreme fulfilment of what is
> meant by 'human being'.[6]

On this view, Jesus is said to have emerged from a genuine historical process like any other human being. But he differs from the
rest of humanity in so far as the process of self-transcendence of
spirit into God, which is the definition of what it means to be
human, has reached fruition in him.

Proceeding christologically 'from below' reverses the way in
which the Church Fathers conceived the problem of Christ's
definition, and it is reasonable to ask whether Rahner has succeeded in reformulating the essential meaning of the traditional
view of the Incarnation, as was his intention, appropriately for a
historically conscious age. Where the exclusivists emphasized the

discontinuity of the person of Christ from the rest of creation, Rahner could be said to have erred the other way, by stressing the continuity at the expense of the radical newness which traditionally Christ was believed to have inaugurated. This means that the uniqueness of Christ has been pin-pointed in the manner to which he differed from the rest of humanity by 'degree' and not 'kind', thus reducing the divine in Christ to the notion of 'perfect humanity'. In terms of orthodox christology this was to fail to make the vital distinction between the activity of God in all of his creation, and that in the Incarnation. Salvation would be the result of the activity of a divinely-inspired good man, and not God himself. Furthermore, the 'degree christology' is deficient in that it posits 'human nature' or 'being human' as the norm for assessing the humanity of Jesus. That is to say, it does not make clear the 'new humanity' which Jesus inaugurates, a notion which is as much part of the christological problem as is the nature of Christ's divinity.

We can make one further observation about this form of christology. It raises the possibility that other men or women, who may be described as Christ-like or filled with the spirit of Christ, can also be incarnations of God to a lesser degree. In the context of the theology of religions this means that it may be possible to believe that God became incarnate in human beings in other cultures for the sake of the salvation of these sections of the human race. This is not to say that God did become incarnate in persons other than Jesus, but for Christians it highlights a deficiency in the traditional doctrine of a unique Incarnation. The reply could be made that this inference from the original formulation is perverse and misses the point of the Incarnation altogether. As Brian Hebblethwaite has said:

> If God himself, in one of the modes of his being, has come into our world in person . . . we cannot suppose he may have done so more than once. For only one man can actually *be* God to us, if God himself is one.[7]

Here Hebblethwaite defends the traditional sense of the Incarnation but advances no argument to support how the doctrine may be comprehended. We shall see shortly how he does this. But at this point we may reflect on the following dilemma. If we wish to acknowledge the genuine humanity of Christ, then it seems impossible to escape the charge of 'degree christology'; but accepting a 'degree christology' has ramifications which hitherto orthodox christology has repudiated. We shall need to penetrate more the issues involved in the current debate over the doctrine of the Incarnation if we are to solve this dilemma.

Before we proceed to this next part of the discussion, however, we need to relate the two christologies I have outlined to the Christian theology of religions. With exclusivism the traditional absoluteness of the Incarnation involved the outright rejection of the non-Christian faiths. But has the shift in the way of formulating the Incarnation in Rahner altered its application in the inclusivist theory? In that Rahner intended to reformulate the traditional meaning of the Incarnation the answer is as we have seen it in Chapter 3: the absolute identification of Jesus with the Logos led to a pre-judgment of the other faiths. But in that Rahner proposes what amounts to a 'degree christology', that sense of pre-judgment is intensified. For what does it mean to proceed christologically 'from below' in relation to other cultures where the understanding of 'what it means to be human' is often so radically different? This form of inclusivism functions by constructing a christology 'from below' in one cultural setting, and then continues to apply it 'from above' in the theology of religions, without seeing the need to enter into some exercise in comparative religion. Employing a christology 'from below' does nothing to mitigate the charge that the issue of truth in religion has been pre-judged by an inclusivist theory; rather, its own case is further damaged. If this is correct, then it means that the acknowledgment of other faiths as forms of communion with God is part of the evidence from which a christology must be constructed. Methodologically, the question of the Incarnation must proceed in tension with the search for a Christian theology of religions.

The ambiguity of the term 'incarnation' is one of the sources of confusion in the current debate about Christ in Christian theological circles. This was amply demonstrated by the ensuing controversy after the publication of *The Myth of God Incarnate* (SCM Press, London 1977).[8] The ambiguity itself is a measure of the distinction, which emerges with the historical-critical method, between the affirmation of the belief and its interpretation. I noted at the beginning of this chapter different linguistic forms in which the doctrine has been clothed. What they amount to is this: that God was personally and uniquely present in Jesus of Nazareth in a sense which cannot be said to be true of any other human being, or founder of a religion. This is the sense which has been intended in this work when I have used the capital 'I' for 'Incarnation'. There is a looser sense to the terms, for which I shall preserve 'incarnation' without the capital. This is generally taken to mean that man's approach to God is through the physical world; and applied to Jesus, that in him we have access to God defined in a special way. But our concern now is with 'Incarnation' and the problems associated with its interpretation. They are well-known and persistent: What is the relationship between God's presence in Jesus and his presence in the rest of creation? How is God's presence in this man to be reconciled with an equal stress on his humanity? We shall consider the problems under several headings – philosophical, theological, historical. These categories overlap, but I distinguish between them simply to facilitate the analysis.

The philosophical challenge to the Incarnation at one time centred on the appropriateness of the terms nature, substance, person, to interpret the unique compatibility of the 'divine' and 'human' in one man. However, most theologians would now agree that belief in the Incarnation is not tied to specific categories of the ancient world. In other words, it is possible to remain agnostic in relation to the particular philosophical framework in which the doctrine has come down to us without jeopardizing the affirmation of faith at the centre. Subsequently, the philosophical issue has now shifted to the question of logical coherence. The challenge is that if 'God' and 'man' delineate two distinct categories of being, how can they be said to be united in one person? If Jesus was a baby in his mother's arms he cannot, it is claimed, have been simultaneously identical with the One who rules the universe. Again, how is it possible for God to remain God and simultaneously be a part of his creation? The logical problem is perhaps the most intractable of all the problems associated with the Incarnation, for 'God' and 'man' are concepts which are not easily defined. It is unlikely, therefore, that we can dub the traditional belief as a sheer contradiction, as talk of a square circle would be straight-forward contradiction. But neither is it sufficient to point out this difficulty in conceptual definition and then go on to claim that God did become man as though there was no need at all for clarification of the logical issue.[9] The difficulty is to know where to place the burden of proof. It is reasonable to claim that this must be shoul-dered by those who wish to uphold some traditional form of the Incarnation, and that a *prima facie* case exists for those who argue that a logical fallacy lies at the heart of it. Furthermore, support for this claim can be adduced from the observation that whenever the doctrine of the Incarnation has been developed in Christian history, beyond the bare God-Man formula, it has always been rejected as heresy. A logical contradiction would preclude any intelligible formulation of the doctrine.

To locate the burden of proof is not to establish an argument, especially the negative one that the doctrine of the Incarnation harbours a logical contradiction. Traditionally, the doctrine has been treated as a paradox, a mystery which ultimately evades logical explanation. Admittedly this does go some way to meet the charge of contradiction, for it has often been pointed out that Christian doctrine contains a number of paradoxes. Moreover, it is possible to speak of paradox not simply as something to live with in theology, but as indicating the litmus test of religious truth. This was in effect the concern of D. M. Baillie's book *God Was in Christ*, which achieved acclaim as a definitive account of this kind of approach. Of all the Christian paradoxes the one which best unfolds the mystery of the Incarnation was the paradox of grace – 'Not I, but the grace of God'. As Baillie wrote:

> this paradox in its fragmentary form in our own Christian lives is a reflection of that perfect union of God and man in the incarnation ... and may therefore be our best clue to the understanding of it.[10]

Baillie's thesis was held by many to have placed paradox firmly on the theological map. Applied to the Incarnation it was seen to treat it not as a problem to be solved, but as a mystery to be preserved. Despite the accolades it won, however, it is difficult to know what was really achieved by it. As there is no logical dis-tinction between a paradox (an apparent contradiction) and a real contradiction, it follows that they can only be distinguished by personal judgment. What is a paradox for one may be a contradiction for another. Baillie himself would not have claimed that his thesis proved anything and it still remains a question whether paradox is the best concept for answering the charges of contradiction.

Baillie's book has been accused of undermining the essence of the Incarnation by equating the manner of God's presence in Christ with that in other men. It is reminiscent of the 'degree christology' we referred to earlier. This may not have been Baillie's intention, but it is questionable whether he has succeeded in achieving anything other than this. However, the real importance of Baillie's book is the shift in the form of the argument which it presents. That is to say, the Incarnation is believed apart from any grounding in the empirical world. The belief is a matter of pure paradox. Though paradox has always played a substantial role as part of the doctrine of the Incarnation, Baillie has made it absolutely central. In the past it was generally held that the doctrine required some basis in empirical reality in order to support its claim. So appeal was made to characteristics in the life of Jesus – for example, his miracles, his self-knowledge as the eternal Son of God, prophecies come to fruition in his life, his claims that he was divine. However, these characteristics of Jesus' life as they are presented in the Gospels now find other explanations, and they are generally thought by most theologians, including those who wish to defend some form of a traditional doctrine, to be invalid as proofs of Christ's divinity. At any rate, it is generally thought that to believe in Christ because he displayed something physically or metaphysically exceptional in his person is to reverse the order of faith. Confession in the divinity of Christ is the conviction that in him one is met by God, not a deduction from divinity-revealing words or events, which would rob Christ of his genuine humanity. With the removal of these kind of arguments, from characteristics in Christ's life as necessarily divinity-revealing, the question arises whether the traditional form of the doctrine has been emptied of content, and now stands in need of revision. This is the problem facing those who have shifted the grounds of the argument in the manner of Baillie's example.

The most likely candidate to be offered currently in response to these kinds of criticism is some version of kenotic theory. Developed at the end of the nineteenth century as a result of growing awareness that the church may have supported a potential docetism in the old formulations of the Incarnation, thus infringing the genuine humanity of Christ, it openly admitted that Christ was limited in his nature, as every other member of the human race is limited. Jesus, before he was anything else, was entirely limited in knowledge, as culturally-determined as any first-century Jew would be, at one with the rest of created humanity. In becoming man God had 'emptied' himself of his divinity and limited himself in an act of utter humility. But this did not mean that Jesus ceased also to be God. He was one with God the Father metaphysically (and therefore, paradoxically).

Kenotic theory was developed in order to overcome the apparent incompatibility of the two natures of Christ, and it has been more or less successful in this. Nevertheless it contains some difficulties which are generally held to be insuperable. Cut from its roots in empirical fact, it is not clear on what grounds the doctrine is being affirmed. As it presupposes the subject of the emptying to be the divine Logos and not man, it does not answer the problem of the pre-existence of Christ, that is, how the historical individuality of Jesus could have been a divine supernatural being. Is it paradox or contradiction? Michael Goulder has argued the problematic nature of the kenotic solution thus:

> This is the challenge to the incarnationalist: *unless some continuity between the Word and Jesus is being asserted, their doctrine is not a paradox but a mystification, not an apparent contradiction but apparent nonsense.*[11]

In reply to this charge Brian Hebblethwaite has written that the continuity in the Incarnation is the action of God in Jesus.[12] But the question remains of how this action manifests itself. In the old doctrine the action was depicted in terms of miracles or oracles said to be divine. But these are disallowed even in the kenotic theory. If Hebblethwaite wishes to see Jesus as the vehicle for God's action, then he is closer than he thinks to those who wish to sever the unique ontological identification of Jesus with God. Yet if he wishes to say more than this, that Jesus' acts were in some sense directly acts of God, then he has not answered Goulder's accusation. Moreover, the real humanity of Jesus will have been violated. The problematic notion of the pre-existence of Christ is, in one form or another, the basic issue in the debate over the Incarnation. We shall return to it when we consider the theological and historical aspects of our enquiry.

Turning now to the theological aspects, these have traditionally centred on the credibility of the belief that one person could embody two natures. The definition of the Council of Chalcedon had set the boundaries of orthodox belief and the theologian's task was to find a way of demonstrating its truth. To some extent this has been the preoccupation also of the preceding section. But the discussion there pointed out some of the changes which have come about in the way of defining the problem, particularly as a result of relinquishing the so-called proofs of Jesus' divinity, as grounds for believing the doctrine itself. As a result of these changes, together with philosophical enquiry concerning the nature of religious language, the theological focus has shifted to the debate over whether the Incarnation is best comprehended as a religious myth, rather than as paradox. The role of myth in Christianity has been recognized at least since D. F. Strauss published his *Life of Jesus* in 1935–6. It came to the forefront of theology dramatically with Bultmann's programme to demythologize the categories of the New Testament and inherited Christian doctrine in order to liberate Christian truth from outmoded expressions, considered no longer meaningful for modern men and women. More recently the publication of *The Myth of God Incarnate* (see p. 112 above) by seven leading British theologians has placed the debate again before the church and the public. What, then, is involved in this proposal that the doctrine of the Incarnation is best comprehended under the heading of myth?

The first part of the problem is to know what is meant by the term 'myth'. As there has been no universally accepted definition, there is liable to be confusion over its application in Christian theology. Strauss himself distinguished between various kinds of myth – historical, poetical, philosophical. The historical myth he defined loosely as 'narratives of real events coloured by the light of antiquity, which confounded the divine and the human, the natural and the supernatural'.[13] In a discussion about Strauss later in the century, Baden Powell defined myth more cogently as 'a doctrine expressed in a narrative form, an abstract moral or spiritual truth dramatized in action and personification; where the object is to enforce faith not in the *parable* but in the *moral*'.[14] Bultmann offered a definition somewhere between the two: 'Mythology is the use of imagery to express the other-worldly in terms of this world and the divine in terms of human life, the other side in terms of this side.'[15] What they all amount to is the recognition that the language of the Incarnation is not meant to be understood literally, but rather belongs in the same group of categories of language as parable, story, image. It is not, strictly speaking, descriptive language, but language designed to evoke a response of faith and commitment in the person who hears or reads it. So, the story that the second person of the Trinity left his place in heaven and came to earth to live the life of a human being for the salvation of the world is not meant to be taken as factual history, but is a story designed to proclaim that the encounter with Jesus was and is, in some sense, an encounter with God. In Jesus we have a point of saving encounter with God, who is to be known as the Father of the universe, and through Jesus' words and pattern of life we can know reconciliation with God. But to treat the language of Incarnation as descriptive narrative is to ask the story to do more work than is possible for it as story, and ultimately there is no escape from the dilemmas which have dogged christological discussion from the beginning. So the argument goes.

The attractions of treating the language of Incarnation as mythological are manifold. In the first place, it resolves the difficulties inherent in the notion of divine intervention. The metaphors of 'sending' and 'becoming' imply that God acts from outside to intervene in a world which, viewed scientifically and historically, is seen normally as a closed web of cause and effect. To speak of Incarnation as myth is one way of separating the christological problem from the interventionist framework of divine action, which is now regarded by the majority of theologians as redundant. It adds nothing, however, to the resolution of the difficulties involved in speaking of divine action itself. But these difficulties persist for any theologian, no matter what views they may espouse about the Incarnation.

In the second place, adoption of the Incarnation as myth solves the intractable problems associated with the concept of pre-existence as it has been applied to Jesus. It is this belief which contradicts the assertion of his full humanity. The ancestry of the notion of pre-existence is mixed, comprising elements of biblical concepts for that which was held to be supremely important as a channel for God's self-revealing activity, and philosophical notions of a mediatorial principle. The New Testament writers who refer to Jesus' pre-existence accord him titles such as Wisdom, Son, Spirit and Word, all of which are attributes of God or agencies of his personal activity, already familiar in the Old Testament. So transforming and total was his impact that a role was attributed to Jesus which rendered him supreme from and for all time in the mediation between God and man. In other words, the human life of Jesus was made the subject of divine personification, a process which we can now only describe as mythological. But as time advanced, Jesus was more readily identified with the divine Word, the Logos, the sole mediator between God and his world, and the agent of God in creation. This had the effect of reversing the myth-making process we have just noted, so that Jesus was identified with a heavenly being, spoken of in various ways as divine, who then became the subject of Jesus' own personality and experience. Treating the myth as theological theory or hypothesis rendered the humanity of Jesus doubtful and had the effect of distorting the true message of the Incarnation. As Geoffrey Lampe has said, 'When Jesus is identified with the pre-existent Son, belief in a true incarnation of God in Jesus is weakened.'[16]

If there are attractions in interpreting the Incarnation as religious myth, this does not mean that it does not pose any questions of its own. In the light of the central role it has played in Christian history it is proper to ask whether this interpretation is sufficient. Sometimes, however, this is asked out of a mistaken sense of thinking that myth is somehow equivalent to falsehood or is simply fictional. But this is to misunderstand the nature and function of myth, which is more akin to linguistic forms such as story or symbol. Nevertheless, to call the doctrine of the Incarnation a myth still leaves open the correct evaluation of the myth in Christian terms. It is in this connection that there can be said to be true or false, appropriate or inappropriate, evaluations of the myth of Incarnation.

Distinguishing between various evaluations of the Incarnation as myth will not be an easy task. In *The Myth of God Incarnate*, Maurice Wiles offers one test of a correct assessment:

> The criterion by which I have been trying to distinguish between true and false interpretations of them might be expressed something like this. There must be some ontological truth corresponding to the central characteristic of the structure of the myth.[17]

He then goes on to specify this ontological correlate at the centre of the myth of Incarnation as the 'potential union of the divine and the human in the life of every man'.[18] Linked to the figure of Jesus, this means being able to affirm historically that he embodied an openness to God and that his life was a parable of the self-giving love of God for the world, two features of the tradition about Jesus which express that unity between the divine and human to which the doctrine points. Another writer, John Knox, also believes the best form of the myth of God Incarnate to be the story of kenosis. Its evaluation lies in the action of God *through* the life of Jesus. Thus the real intention of the notion of pre-existence applied to Jesus was the conviction

> that God, the Father Almighty, Maker of the heavens and the earth, was back of, present in, and acting through the whole event of which the human life of Jesus was the centre.[19]

Finally we may cite John Robinson as someone for whom the correct interpretation of the New Testament is the touchstone of truth about the Incarnation:

> To register the conviction that in this man was fulfilled and embodied the meaning of God reaching back to the very beginning, they proclaim him as his Word, his Wisdom, his Image, his Son, from all eternity.[20]

But the question remains: are these evaluations of the myth of Incarnation sufficient to preserve the initiative of God in Jesus which is the real power of the doctrine? It is easy to see how many may feel disquiet at the radical loosening of the bonds of ontological identity between God and Jesus that they entail. Certainly there are those for whom the depiction of the Incarnation as myth is correct in so far as it rejects interventionist notions of God's activity or even the pre-existence of Jesus, but who would be reluctant to sever the unique bond between God and Jesus, since this is held to be the true heritage of Christian truth. Christian experience, it has been argued, dictates that some ontological identity between God and Jesus needs to be retained, otherwise the distinctive religious and moral power of Christian faith will have been surrendered. What is the force of this objection to the interpretation of the Incarnation as myth?

Brian Hebblethwaite, in particular, points to two features of Christian experience which he believes demand that God and Jesus be identified in a more direct way than the understanding of myth allows. The first is the personal nature of the encounter of God in Christ, and the second is the belief that as a result of the cross God in Christ has taken responsibility for the world's evil. As he has said:

> The moral and religious significance of Christ's life and death depends on his being God in person.[21]

Hebblethwaite would admit that he is not attempting to argue from value to truth, but that the moral and religious value discerned in the doctrine may be an indication or pointer to its truth. This may be accepted, yet the real question is whether Hebblethwaite's argument has the force he believes it to have. In reply to Hebblethwaite, Keith Ward has shown how these values inherent in the traditional doctrine can be equally well, and in some respects more potently discerned in an interpretation of the Incarnation which disavows the ontological linkage.[22] The sense of personal encounter with God is equally a feature of, say, the citations from Knox, Robinson and Wiles given above. Furthermore, it has the advantage, as Ward points out, of saving us from obscurity when the identity between God and Jesus is stressed unnecessarily. On any account of Incarnation God still remains infinite and transcendent as he is conceived under the human form of Jesus, and it is unorthodox to say that Jesus *is* God. On the moral point, it is necessary to say that God must suffer with all his creation and not just in one man, as Hebblethwaite maintains, if he is to share the moral responsibility for the world's evil. Again, the advantage of the alternative view is that it enables the cross of Christ to stand as the 'classic instance' of God's involvement in suffering, rather than as the anomalous exception which would limit that involvement to one man. Hebblethwaite is more unduly worried than he need be by what he conceives as a loss to the moral and religious impact of the Incarnation if it is not interpreted along ontological lines. For as Ward has made clear:

> On both accounts, what he is really opposing is a particular Patristic doctrine of God – namely, that God is not personal (being Pure Being, beyond all categories) and that God is impassible.[23]

Hebblethwaite, it seems, is still working with a conceptual framework of substance-nature-person, so that the only christological alternatives are either 'Jesus as inspired man' or 'Jesus as of the same substance as God the Father'. As a way out of the impasse Ward further suggests that we take more seriously the suggestion that God is 'a transcendent source of being and value' and not a substance. On this view the doctrine of the Incarnation receives a different evaluation:

> Perhaps we can then see Jesus in his necessarily unique historical context as a focal point within the whole history of the world, at which a paradigm model for transcendence arises.[24]

This way of stating the doctrine is close to the Knox, Robinson and Wiles view, and its value lies in corroborating the claims of those who wish to develop the meaning of the Incarnation as myth in a positive direction. At least it allays the fears of those who are suspicious of viewing christology in this way, that it empties the doctrine of the Incarnation of all content. In the Christian theology of religions Ward's suggestions point in the direction of the inclusivist theory exemplified by Robinson and Küng. We shall pick up Ward's suggestion at a later stage in the discussion when we consider the relative merits of these inclusivist theories in conjunction with a christological perspective of this kind. We turn now to consider the historical problems associated with the doctrine of the Incarnation.

A belief which proposes that one person was related to the God of the universe and history in a unique manner and form cannot escape an encounter with modern changes in historical understanding. In fact this encounter had dominated theological debate at least since the Enlightenment. But engagement with historical studies is notoriously a minefield, especially in relation to the Incarnation. There are those for whom the evidence of scripture and Christian witness throughout the ages can be marshalled to support some traditional account of the doctrine; and at the other end of the spectrum there are those for whom the evidence does not necessarily add up in the way the tradition has always assumed. There are also those for whom the encounter with history is strictly limited in its application to the work of the theologian proper. We shall consider some of the historical problems associated with the Incarnation under two headings: 'What is the importance of a historically reconstructed picture of Jesus?', and 'How do we interpret the New Testament evidence generally in relation to Jesus?' In all of this it is important to remember that nothing is proved or disproved about the Incarnation purely as a result of the encounter with history. The effect will be, however, to give shape to a debate, and to try and discern where the impact of history on christology really lies.

That Jesus was the fount of a radical religious movement in the first century is beyond the doubt of the majority of New Testament scholars today. No one now entertains the idea, which has been submitted from time to time, that the figure of Jesus was wholly the construct of the primitive church based on material drawn from the Hellenistic world and the religious imagination. However, the exact nature of the creative impact of Jesus, and his own specific contribution to the rise of the new religion, is much more a matter of dispute. Before the rise of the modern historical method, the text of scripture was accepted as divinely guaranteed and the life of Jesus simply corresponded to a literal reading of the text. The rise of biblical criticism, however, has had the effect of driving a wedge between the text and the divine guarantee, and so has reduced the certainty which our forebears enjoyed concerning the life of Jesus. Nevertheless, this has not foreclosed the possibility of a portrayal of the figure of Jesus in a more general outline. In this the so-called 'new quest for the historical Jesus' has done much to restore confidence in what can be affirmed about Jesus. We may not know in detail Jesus' life, but critical investigation of the sources reveals a figure about whom some general characteristics can be affirmed. Even those who are less certain about the results of the 'new quest' are prepared to acknowledge that it is possible to discern in the New Testament, for all its diverse witness, a general impression of what Jesus must have taught and preached. But more crucial than what can be known concerning Jesus' life is the importance which attaches to this kind of historical judgment about him, made after critical investigation of the sources. For it answers the central question implied in the whole search for the 'Jesus of history'. That is to say, if a Christian faith-judgment about Jesus is to be justified, it must include some historical knowledge which is consistent with the faith-judgment itself. Precisely what form that faith will take, whether Jesus will be seen as ontologically or mythologically God Incarnate, will depend on many factors. But the necessity for some knowledge of Jesus, even of a very general kind, is indispensable to any form of Christian faith. For instance it would not be appropriate to declare faith in Jesus if it was known that he was a deceiver or seeker after his own glory. Of course the level of tolerance for the credibility of the gap between the knowledge and the faith will vary from writer to writer. And there is always the danger that the historical knowledge of Jesus discerned by the critical study will be just sufficient to 'fit' what is required anyway by this approach to the Christian faith. Such, for example, was George Tyrrell's conclusion at the beginning of this century, regarding Harnack's view of Jesus that, as he said, 'the Christ (he) sees looking back through nineteen centuries of Catholic darkness, is only the reflection of a liberal Protestant face, seen at the bottom of a deep well'.[25] However, given this warning, if it can be affirmed, on the basis of the critical historical investigation of the sources, that the gap between 'history' and 'faith' is not intolerable, then we have reached the necessary understanding concerning the 'Jesus of history' question. We may more or less agree with Edward Schillebeeckx:

> Jesus was not proclaimed to be the Christ despite or apart from what he really was in history.[26]

This, we may say, is the result of faith seeking historical understanding where 'historical enquiry is essential for the access of faith to the authentic gospel'.[27]

The 'Jesus of history' is only one component of the christological question. If there is restored confidence, albeit minimal for some, in what can be known about the historical figure, there still remains the consideration of the other pole of the relationship between the figure and the church's proclaimed faith about him down the ages, the so-called 'Christ of faith'. At stake here is the more general interpretation of Jesus and the impact he made as it is recorded in the New Testament. A fair question would be: to what extent does the New Testament as a whole point in the direction of the Incarnation which orthodoxy subsequently established? Again, there is much diversity among scholars as to the correct answer. However, all would agree that the evidence of scripture witnesses in a much less direct sense to the later doctrine than used to be assumed. It is no longer permissible to read the Fourth Gospel texts which equate Jesus and God – for example, 'I and the Father are one', and 'Before Abraham was I am' – as verbatim from the mouth of Jesus himself. How Jesus understood himself is extremely difficult to know, and need not be pursued here. A more fruitful line of enquiry in biblical research has been to examine the titles honouring Jesus. He is interpreted variously as eschatological prophet, Messiah, Son of Man, Son of God, Wisdom, Word, Lord. Some of the titles, for example Messiah or Son of God, reflect the sense that Jesus is the one sent by God to do God's work, to act and speak on God's behalf. Other titles, for example Wisdom or Lord, reflect a more all-embracing effect than this, carrying the conviction that to be in the presence of Jesus was equivalent to being in the presence of God. Much has been gained by this approach. But in more recent years New Testament scholarship has shifted its gaze away from the titles themselves, to the overall manner in which the different writers speak about Jesus. We have become increasingly aware of the differing theological concerns and outlooks which dominated the writers' perspectives, so that Jesus is seen to speak and act largely in accordance with these concerns. As a result of these kinds of study the real question which we need to ask is this: without reading back into the New Testament the doctrine of later ages, what is the best way of interpreting the diverse witness to Jesus in order to assist in formulating a belief about him today? Again, more than one view is possible in answer to this question. In order to illustrate two very different interpretations of the New Testament evidence, one can cite the work of two New Testament scholars, J. L. Houlden and C. F. D. Moule. The former believes that the essential thing about Jesus was the transformed belief in God to which he gave rise:

> Such a theology might be best described as a transformed monotheism: belief in a God to whom Jesus had given colour, shape and definition, and with whom the immensely creative impact of Jesus has opened up a new style of relationship.[28]

For this writer the descriptions of Jesus are not evidence of Jesus' divinity so much as 'projections' in objective language deriving from basic religious experience of which Jesus was the source. So when Jesus is viewed as the pre-existent agent in creation by some writers, the description reflects the transformed attitude to the whole of the created world which the new awareness of God, derived from Jesus, brought with it. But treat the language as somehow more literal than that and we run into all the familiar problems surrounding the notion of pre-existence. Conversely, Moule wishes to claim that Jesus was not only interpreted by the New Testament writers as transcendent but was also *experienced* as such. In reply to Houlden he writes:

> It is not just that, owing (somehow) to Jesus, they found new life; it is that they discovered in Jesus himself, alive and present, a divine dimension such that he must always and eternally have existed in it.[29]

This leads Moule to affirm pre-existence as necessary for christology today if we are to be true to the New Testament witness at all. For Houlden, however, this is required more than anything by faithfulness to the evidence of scripture. Our problem is in knowing how to assess the two positions and the ambiguity which such discrepant interpretations of the New Testament imply. As historical enquiry is never free from pre-suppositions, it may be that both writers are in danger of selecting those elements of the text which fit their case. On the one hand, Houlden is in danger of seeing only what his empiricist approach allows. On the other hand, Moule is in danger of reading the New Testament text through the eyes of later orthodoxy. Is there a way of resolving this dispute? Perhaps one way suggests itself if we examine the notion of pre-existence in the context of the Judaism of the time. Preexistence was often attributed to that which mediated or disclosed the goodness and truth of God. This elevating process was applied above all to the Jewish Law, seen as God's gift for the strengthening of his people's relationship with him. In this light is it not more reasonable to see the pre-existence of Jesus as more the product of this kind of elevating process than as anything ontological in his nature, understandable at the time but only confusing now? If this is granted, then a major obstacle, as Moule partially admits pre-existence to be, will have been overcome. After that the problem of christology can only be resolved in relation to the wider issues associated with it.

I have outlined a number of criticisms which have been applied to the doctrine of the Incarnation in recent years. In one sense they are not new, and in essence can be seen to date from the rise of the historical-critical study of scripture. They have come into sharp focus only now as a result of the sustained critical study itself. It will be clear from the above discussion that no clear-cut arguments can be adduced to support either the upholders of a traditional sense of the Incarnation or their critics. Judgment can be made only after examining a host of issues. The critique from the en-counter with history in particular raises the general question of whether the Incarnation is an evaluation of the person of Jesus appropriate for a past era, but not binding on all subsequent eras. This question would be real also for those who adhere to the Incarnation as a purely metaphysical doctrine, seeming to by-pass any hard encounter with history. If we now judge that the criticisms of the Incarnation which hold that Jesus is ontologically one with God, unlike any other human being, are sufficient cumulatively to warrant a reformulation in our understanding, this does not mean that Christianity as a way of response to God and his purposes has been dismantled. Theology is not christology. Critical study may often appear negative, but it need not necessarily be so. True critical study ought to point towards a positive reappraisal in addi-tion to raising questions about past forms of belief. I have already hinted at the forms such a re-appraisal is likely to take, and now turn to examine them in more detail.

The important shift which the newer christologies make is away from concentrating exclusively on the person of Christ, and the puzzle posed by viewing him as both divine and human, to talk of what can broadly be termed the action of God in Christ. At root it is the total impact of Jesus, the so-called 'Christ-event', and the intention of the Father's will through it that makes him unique. Jesus is accepted as fully a human being with all the limitations of knowledge and cultural relatedness that that involves. The difference with him is that through this one man, God has acted in such a way as to provide a path of reconciliation with God. The action and presence of God is seen as all of a piece with Jesus' human action and presence, which is itself the vehicle for the saving work of God. Jesus' divinity is more a quality of his role in opening up access to God the Father's love and grace than, strictly speaking, of his personal nature. But in that we believe his message to have been embodied in his person, Jesus' role does indeed spring out of his person. To cite some further words from John Knox:

> For this divinity consists in the central and integral involvement of Jesus's human life in God's supremely redemptive action and the pervasive presence of God's supremely redemptive action in his human life.[30]

It is not that God enters into the human life of Jesus from outside, so to speak, but that in his human life Jesus 'shapes' a new understanding of the ways of God in the world. In the words of an Indian writer, Vengal Chakkarai, who echoes the citation from Houlden above:

> We see God with the face of Jesus . . . Whom we call God stands behind Jesus, and it is Jesus who gives, as it were, colour, light and *rupa* (form) to God.[31]

Yet precisely because Jesus makes plain the ways of God in and for the world, he can be said to initiate a 'new humanity'. Jesus is 'important', to borrow a term from process theology, not because he possesses any extra divine quality which is absent from other human beings, but because he focusses in himself the purposes of God for the world and the human response which God is continually, so I believe, working to elicit.

The advantages of this action-christology, as we might call it, are legion. First, it takes seriously the genuine historical nature of Jesus, who is, as the Epistle to the Hebrews says, 'chosen from among men' in order to 'act on behalf of men in relation to God'

(5.1). Second, it avoids the problems of incoherence in the language of pre-existence. This can now be admitted as frankly 'mythological'. Third, it overcomes the impasse, noted by Ward, of 'Jesus as divinely-inspired prophet' versus 'Jesus as of the same substance as the Father'. Jesus was not *merely* (as is sometimes said pejoratively) divinely-inspired, but he was God given exegesis (John 1.18), so that to have been in his presence was to have been in God's presence. There is an equivalence between God and Jesus in terms of value and function. The real significance of Jesus lies in that through his being 'at the human level' he brings to completion 'at the spiritual level' the purposes of God from the beginning. Fourth, the 'importance' of the process theologians helps to overcome the subjective versus objective polarization in the apprehension of Jesus. In process thought something is 'important' when it becomes a key to our understanding. An event can have this quality because it compels our attention and provides an occasion for organizing our experience in a new way. The objectivity lies in the reality of what is being offered through the event, and the subjectivity lies in the realization that until we respond, the offer remains of no consequence. This is a refusal to speak of divine action in any context other than that of experienced response. Fifth, it shows up the 'degree' versus 'kind' christology I mentioned earlier as false. Jesus is not unique because he represents perfected humanity or because he displays qualities of saintliness surpassing any other human being. Most probably he did display these qualities in his person and they were responsible for compelling people to find him 'important' in the first place. But of themselves they are not the reason for calling Jesus 'important' theologically. Like the inspiration-substance debate it rests on outmoded categories of the ancient world.

The disadvantage with action-christology is precisely that it speaks of divine action at a time when it is extremely difficult to know the meaning of 'act of God' itself. However, the problem is not wholly insuperable. One example of the attempt to say what constitutes divine action comes from the perspective of process theology which I have already mentioned. God is said to act in the affairs of the world through loving persuasion, by 'aim', 'lure' and 'mutual prehension'. These are technical terms which specify how God 'can allow the fullest freedom to the creature. Yet not simply in spite of, but through and by means of, that freedom he can secure through free consent the accomplishment of his purpose . . .'[32] God's action in Jesus was in no sense different from his action in the rest of creation, except in that through Jesus' particular 'aim', 'lure' and 'prehension' he has become 'important', and thereby makes a difference in the relationship between man and God. Essentially what was made manifest through the 'Christ-event' is the loving action of God, which is exercised whenever love is practised in the world, but was focussed in the events of Jesus. The love of God was congruous, we may say, with the love of Jesus, but it did not replace it. On this view, therefore, the metaphysical bond between Jesus and God was moral, once we grasp the point that the love of God is the basis of the life of the universe. Pittenger called this a 'christianization of ontology'.[33] But all of this is one particular model for understanding divine action and we need not pursue it further here. The problem of divine action is distinguishable from the problem of christology, though related to it. And there is much more work for theologians to do in this connection, no matter what account they may wish to give of the Incarnation.

The interpretation I have given of the Incarnation will doubtless appear to many, in spite of the advantages I have listed, 'reductionist' or insufficient to explain the initiative of God that faith believes was at work in Jesus. This would be too harsh a judgment for the reasons I have adduced. I find any other account unable to deal honestly with Jesus' humanity and the critical-historical investigations of the New Testament. The tension between the old and new approaches can be illustrated by reference to any recent work in christology. But perhaps the whole debate is nowhere more admirably encapsulated than in Edward Schillebeeckx's two books, *Jesus* (Collins, London 1979) and *Christ* (SCM Press, London 1980). It is worth reflecting a little on these two works before moving on to examine the place of the newer christology in the Christian theology of religions.

In his first book, *Jesus*, Schillebeeckx has shown how Christian faith in Jesus may be grounded in a critical handling of the Gospels. Not that he believed historical enquiry could demonstrate or prove faith; its role was to sift the evidence in order to show how a Christian interpretation, as opposed to any other, is consistent with it. Schillebeeckx fully recognized the differences in culture and understanding between the time of Jesus and now, and was alert to the anachronism of reading the New Testament from the standpoint of later orthodoxy. His conclusion was similar to what I have said above:

> Jesus is from God and for his fellow-men, he is God's gift to all people: this is the New Testament's final view . . .[34]

Schillebeeckx realized, however, that in another setting this may be expressed differently. The refusal to separate Jesus' message from his person led Schillebeeckx to endorse the church fathers' insistence on forging an ontological bond between Jesus and his heavenly Father. Dissociating himself from the patristic method he believed this was entirely possible to argue 'from below': 'In his humanity Jesus is so intimately "of the Father" that by virtue of this very intimacy he is "Son of God".'[35] Consequently, the substance and action christologies which I have presented as incompatible, appeared united in Schillebeeckx's final conclusion, though he recognized the ultimate impossibility of adequately stating the divine sonship of Jesus:

> Through his historical self-giving, accepted by the Father, Jesus has shown us who God is: a *Deus humanissimus*. How the man Jesus can be for us at the same time the form and aspect of a divine 'person', the Son . . . is . . . a mystery unfathomable beyond this point.[36]

Schillebeeckx has shown here how christology derives from, and ought not to be considered apart from, soteriology. This rescues much traditional christology from abstractions. Nevertheless, Schillebeeckx is not wholly unambiguous. Is the formulation of Jesus as a 'divine "person", the Son' a retreat into the older language and thought-forms, or does it genuinely follow from the need to hold together Jesus' message and his person? I noted above that it is misleading to speak of divine action, and above all divine action in Jesus, in any context other than that of its experienced response. In principle Schillebeeckx accepted this, and he made it abundantly clear in his second volume, *Christ*: 'The offer of grace and the answer of faith are the two facets of one and the same rich reality.'[37] This implied that for the Christian faith to apply in the

modern world, the analysis of the offer of grace, the central Christian experience, must be linked with an analysis of both the historical
circumstances in which it first took root and the very different
circumstances to which it is directed now. Holding these two
concerns together, Schillebeeckx has shown how the experience of
God's grace is experienced not only when man is turned towards
God in prayer, but also in relationships between human beings
and in the structures of society. In this last regard salvation, he
believed, is concerned with overcoming of man's experience of
despair and meaninglessness, especially in the face of suffering and
failure. His conclusion was simple but challenging nonetheless;
salvation consists in:

> being at the disposal of others, losing oneself to others and
> within this 'conversion' also working through anonymous struc-
> tures for the happiness, the goodness and the truth of mankind.
> This way of life, born of grace, provides a real possibility for a
> very personal encounter with God, who is then experienced as
> the source of all happiness and salvation, the source of all
> joy . . .
>   This is existing for others and thus for *the* Other, the wholly
> intimate and near yet 'transcendent God', with whom Jesus
> made us familiar.[38]

The emphasis of Schillebeeckx here is salutary for christology.
Jesus is significant for the 'way of life, born of grace', which he
initiated, or as I should prefer to say, which God initiated through
him. If salvation is understood, as it is in this passage, in terms of
personal relationship with the ' "transcendent God", with whom
Jesus has made us familiar', then it is not essential to establish that
a union existed between the divine and human in Jesus of a kind
uniquely different from that in other human beings. What this
implies is that the union represents the 'focus' or 'paradigm' of the
union between man and God which we anticipate as the intended
goal of salvation. Expressed in this way, both the initiative of God's
action in Jesus and the human response in faith are preserved. If
Schillebeeckx intends the 'uniqueness' of Jesus to have been more
than this, then this can only confuse the issue. In answer to his
critics of *Jesus* and *Christ*, Schillebeeckx wrote that 'in the definition of what he is, the man Jesus is indeed connected with the

nature of God'.[39] I have attempted to say something similar, though the connection between Jesus and the nature of God has been stipulated more in moral terms, of 'love in action', rather than in pure ontological terms. Jesus was incarnate in that he embodied not only a profound human response to God, that openness to God necessary for the life of faith, but also the turning of God towards man in his distress and need of salvation. Both aspects are expressive of that union between the divine and the human to which the doctrine of the Incarnation points, and both are firmly embedded in the gospel traditions as characteristics of Jesus' own life.

Our task in this chapter is the consideration not only of the doctrine of Christ, but also of the place of that doctrine in the Christian theologies of religions. Calling the Incarnation a myth does not automatically settle the question of Christianty's relation to the other faiths. In principle it does not even rule out the exclusivist theory, though I know of no theory which does evaluate the Incarnation as myth in an exclusivist direction. Moreover, it would be extremely difficult to know what the grounds would be for such an evaluation once the 'literal' understanding of the Incarnation has been abandoned. In the context of the Christian theology of religions, what is at stake is the 'finality' of Christ, a notion which is linked with, though distinguishable from, the Incarnation. Having been first established in the context of the eschatological 'philosophy of history' of first-century Judaism, it then became a function of the Incarnation. But if the Jewish eschatology is no longer applicable,[40] given the revolution in historical thinking, and the Incarnation is understood as myth, what meaning can be attached to the doctrine of Christ's finality? Two different ways forward have been suggested, and we turn now to consider both. We shall examine the place of an action-christology in both the 'open' inclusivist theory of John Robinson and the pluralist theory of John Hick.

In his *Truth is Two-Eyed* Robinson quoted the work of Norman Pittenger, whose position approximated to Robinson's own:

For myself, I believe that the finality of Christ is nothing other than his decisive disclosure that God is suffering, saving, and ecstatic love. Surely you cannot get anything more final than that. But there can be many different approaches to this, many different paths to its realization, many different intimations, adumbrations, and preparations.[41]

Yet, unlike Pittenger, Robinson was aware that for inclusivism to 'work' it could not avoid entering the 'field of invidious comparisons with other religions'.[42] The test of Jesus as the 'decisive disclosure' of God was the ability of the theology which stems from him to deal adequately with the features of human experience that are inimical to religious faith. He listed the realities of suffering, evil, sin, the feminine and the impersonal as examples of such features. In principle he believed that Christ in his 'decisive disclosure' does deal more profoundly with these elements than do other faiths. Furthermore, it enabled Robinson to say that Christ does not disclose every religious truth, but that he is 'the best clue', and therefore Christians can be open to other traditions which 'can clarify, complete and correct "the vision of Christ that I do see" '.[43]

We noted in the general discussion of Robinson's version of inclusivism (see above, pp. 64ff.) that there is a tension at the heart of his theory: how far does the conviction that Jesus is 'decisive' contradict the claim of the book's title that 'truth is two-eyed'? On the one hand, he veers towards pluralism when he recognizes the genuine spirituality of other faiths:

> If Jesus is the Christ, if, in other words, *God* is to be met in his reconciling the world to himself, and if Krishna or any other figure is an *avatara* of the 'All-highest Brahman', 'the God of gods', then in the last analysis we must be dealing with the same *Logos*, the same Christ. To rest with an ultimate pluralism at this point is intolerable.[44]

This, we may say, is an expression of the belief that 'truth is two-eyed'. On the other hand, Robinson dissents from the implication of such a belief when he disagrees with John Hick's judgment in *The Myth of God Incarnate* (p. 176), that if the gospel had travelled east instead of west the apprehension of the spiritual significance of Jesus in terms of, say, a divine avatar, would have been a legitimate and appropriate apprehension of the same reality. This reflects Robinson's concern to retain Jesus as 'decisive'. There may be a genuine contradiction here, sufficient to jeopardize Robinson's inclusivist approach. Pittenger, in his *Christology Reconsidered*, made it quite clear that 'decisiveness' cannot arise from a comparative study of religions but is an expression of one's own faith-commitment.[45] Hence he echoes the Vatican II inclusivists when he says that it is Christ who 'can crown and correct and complete that of God which elsewhere has been revealed'.[46] This is opposed to Robinson, who is aware that this way of stating the matter pre-judges the issue of truth. In an age when Christians are becoming more conscious of the relative isolation of cultures in the past, and christology is 'from below', the 'decisiveness' of Christ, he believes, can only be affirmed in conjunction with some comparison of religious beliefs. But whether such comparative work can be done to meet these ends is a large question, and many think it is not very plausible. If it can be done, then it is certainly too early to know what the outcome may be. Robinson is in danger of pre-judging the issue in a more subtle guise. In so far as he seeks to formulate an inclusivist theory as a *via media* between the narrow exclusivist and relativizing pluralist positions, as he sees them, his account takes more seriously the impact of historical studies on both the interpretation of the Incarnation and the relation of Christianity to the other faiths in respect of religious truth. But at this stage in the dialogue between religions, to hold on to Christ as 'decisive' in the sense which Robinson implies is as much an act of faith as a judgment of theology.

The alternative theory in the theology of religions which employs an action-christology is pluralism. I have defended this approach as the most positive Christian response to the encounter between Christianity and the world faiths. From a christological perspective it accepts the Incarnation in its traditional account of the descent of the Son of God to earth as mythological. Along with Robinson it is aware that Christian identity is at risk if viewing the Incarnation in this way minimizes the significance of the union between God and man in Jesus for the relationship between God and man now. But no such minimizing is entailed in the pluralist theory; Jesus is still 'decisive'. However, unlike Robinson's approach, Jesus' 'decisiveness' is viewed as primarily related to those who have received the light of God through him, and not because he is the predetermined focus for all the light everywhere revealed in the world. As an originating *locus* of transcendent vision and human transformation Jesus of course is a figure of universal significance, but not unsurpassably or indispensably so.

This would still seem to many an unacceptable reduction of the real normativity of Christ, or of that finality which has tradition-ally belonged at the heart of Christian faith. That objection is too harsh a judgment in the light of the present encounter between faiths, and it reflects a lack of historical sense which should be impossible for Christians to ignore. The objections to it can be met in terms such as these:

> We have to present Jesus and the Christian life in a way com-patible with our new recognition of the validity of the other great world faiths . . . The Christian gift to the world is Jesus, the 'largely unknown man of Nazareth' whose impact has nevertheless created such powerful images in men's minds that he is for millions the way, the truth and the life. Within the varying cultures and changing circumstances of history he can still create fresh images and can become men's lord and liberator in yet further ways.[47]

In this theory, therefore, the spiritual profundity of Christianity has not been usurped, any more than the spiritual gifts within other faiths have been pre-judged. The universal intention and destiny of Christian faith ought to be exercised in an open dialogue. This should avoid syncretism, allow all members to foster the preservation of their own tradition as an authentic expression of genuine religious experience, be prepared to accept that some religious insights are poor or inadequate, and seek for ways in which religious beliefs can be viewed as complementary. Further-more, this does not entail that Christ is being judged by a prior conception of God not found in the Christian tradition, as Lesslie Newbigin believes.[48] It is allowing that the person of Jesus, and the experience of relationship with God which he initiated, can make it own contribution to the dialogue, challenging in its own way the wider religious experience of mankind. Jesus would still remain central for Christian faith. But the adherents of the other faiths ought also to be allowed to make their own distinct contribution to the dialogue. In this way the dialogue carries implications for christology, as Frances Young has said:

What we make of Christ cannot be considered without reference to our total experience of God's world, a world in which everything is coloured by the specific particularities of individuals, cultures, historical circumstances and so on.[49]

Viewing Jesus in this way not only rescues Christianity from embarrassment in an age of radical historical consciousness: it also releases him to make his impact afresh in the dialogue, at the important level of religious experience.

6

A QUESTION OF TRUTH

Christianity has never been understood merely as an abstract faith or an esoteric theory in a sense which implies a disjunction between divine revelation and historical happenings. On the contrary, it has always been thought that in this particular faith theological theory and historical enquiry belong together as two parts of a symbiotic whole. This means therefore that Christian theology cannot remain indifferent to changes in historical knowledge. For some time now the church's appropriation of its own theological past has been undergoing profound changes as a result of a sharpened historical scholarship developed since the Enlightenment. But the impact of historical study is even more profound than raising questions about the relation between the church and its theological past. For if Christian theology is so wedded to historical enquiry, then it must sooner or later wrestle with the accumulated knowledge of the world faiths, now at our fingertips, as part of its theological data. Commitment to history means commitment to that which has existed in history as material for theological reflection. The existence of the ancient non-Christian faiths, some of which have flourished for many centuries before Christianity, poses a major problem for a faith which views all history as lying within God's providential care and yet which sees its own history as absolute or final. The Christian theological response to the existence of other faiths proclaiming different ways of salvation is only just beginning to be taken seriously. Movement towards dialogue as the appropriate mode of relationship is one indication of the serious-ness with which the task is being appreciated by Christian theo-logians. Yet the response has begun sufficiently for there to be

already a range of theories in the field. Variety of response, however, does not mean that there are an endless number of positions.
There is a pattern within the variety which I have analysed typo-
logically as three-fold in the terms exclusivism, inclusivism, and
pluralism. Moreover, I have done this in the full realization that
classifying phenomena into theoretical types inevitably simplifies
our subject as this exists concretely. It is apt to miss the special and
particular nuances of any one position in the bid to categorize. I
have tried to compensate for this by deliberately bringing out the
diversity of opinion within each theoretical type. The threefold
typology is valid, I believe, in so far as it helps to discriminate
broadly between the available options in the Christian theology of
religions, and to assist understanding of the issues with which they
are concerned. In the final analysis any typology is simply an aid to
understanding the truth and ought not to pose as the truth itself.

Of the three theoretical types, I have given reasons why the
pluralist argument is the most profitable for evaluating the relation
between the Christian and the other faiths in the light of all the
evidence. That this represents something of a bold departure from
the general inherited Christian theorizing on the matter cannot be
gainsaid. In fact most scholars today probably feel instinctively
drawn towards some version of exclusivism or inclusivism, given
the venerable status of these positions in Christian history. Also, a
nervousness about recasting our interpretation of the Incarnation,
entailed by the pluralist position, leads many to dismiss it as less
than Christian in approach. Nevertheless, pluralism has made
some ground in Christian theology, becoming one more variant in
the total Christian understanding of human religious experience.
It may not have a solid historical pedigree, but that is no reason
for abandoning it *a priori*, only for subjecting it to searching
criticism. If the criticism can be met with good argument, and full
account of the dynamic nature of the Christian tradition, which
has seen many innovations, is taken, then pluralism can be viewed
as a respectable option in the Christian theology of religions.

The starting-point for the pluralist theory is the validity of the
notion of religious experience, which is embodied in various ways
in the religious traditions of the world. Valued as an authentic
encounter with the divine, the experience is describable and is
characterized differently within the traditions. Christians partici-

pate in the religious life of mankind as one strand of faith alongside others. But we have been careful to stress that this framework does not imply that all faiths are equally true or are the same, with the consequence that the cognitive clashes between traditions can be ignored or are irrelevant. To this matter I shall return below. I wish now to substantiate further the argument for pluralism in the Christian theology of religions by demonstrating why reflection on the encounter between the faiths must proceed from a notion of religious experience. The argument employs insights from a sociological perspective and reflects on the influence of the so-called modern secular consciousness, which is spreading to all parts of the world, on the *authority* of religious traditions.

Historians and sociologists have been assessing throughout the modern period the momentous effects on religious institutions of the process which has become known in general terms as secularization. In particular, they have pointed to the breakdown in the authoritative hold that traditional patterns of religious belief and practice have on individuals and groups. Whereas the world was once thought to rest largely in the hands of the gods or fate, a belief authoritatively bolstered by an elaborate theology and by close-knit social structures, modern men and women are much more likely to experience the world as the arena where they must take responsibility themselves for shaping and building the world out of their own resources and technical capability. Responsibility for living, we may say, has passed out of the hands of fate or the gods, and therefore out of the hands of the guardians of tradition also, into the hands of men and women themselves. The crisis which this entails for the authority of religious belief and practice is immense, and theologians have been attempting to come to terms with it for a number of years. Related to this process of secularization is the awareness of a plurality of religious and secular world-views confronting the individual. When the unquestioned authority of a tradition declines, the large and difficult task which faces an individual is how to assess the wide range of different philosophies and world-views that can be paraded before him. Further, even if the participant in this process has not had first-hand experience of all the major philosophies of the world (how could he, anyway?), it is possible for him to have second-hand access through contacts with neighbours who hold an outlook at variance with his own, or through experiences of world travel, or through books of comparative religion and philosophy. The sociologist Peter Berger has termed this whole situation 'the heretical imperative'. Thus:

> *For premodern man, heresy is a possibility – usually a rather remote one; for modern man, heresy typically becomes a necessity. Or again, modernity creates a new situation in which picking and choosing becomes an imperative.*[1]

Etymologically, 'heresy' simply means the making of choices, and in a world where the theological and socially institutionalized authoritative backing – termed 'the plausibility structures' in sociological jargon – for any religious tradition cannot be taken for granted, living 'heretically' has become a matter of fact. We may perhaps count Berger over-enthusiastic in his estimate of the degree to which men and women actually experience the 'heretical imperative'; nevertheless we may expect it will become more and more a normal part of the conscious reflections of most people. As it is, at the theoretical level it has become something which is difficult to refute. In such circumstances, for religious traditions to survive they must seek to understand and appropriate the underlying experiences at the roots of their respective traditions. Again, Berger expresses this aspect of the effect of pluralization:

> It follows that the modern situation, with its weakened hold of religious tradition over the consciousness of individuals, must lead to much more deliberate reflection about the character and the evidential status of religious experience.[2]

If Berger is correct in this judgment, then the notion of religious experience is the single and most profitable concept in theological reflection, assuming the secularization and pluralization premises. It will be most profitable for any one religion (Christianity included), and we may expect therefore that it will be the starting-point for the theological reflection involved in the encounter between religions. This is what I have contended in the theory I have called pluralism in the Christian theology of religions.

It is possible to follow Berger's analysis a little further in order to substantiate the pluralist theory. Given the 'heretical imperative' premise, Berger considers the reaction to this feature of contemporary experience in three Protestant theologians: Barth,

Bultmann, and Schleiermacher. Our interest now is in what Berger says about Barth's theological method in relation to the relativizing force of modern socio-historical thought. In the face of the 'heretical imperative' Barth's procedure was to reject the analysis as having anything binding to say for the Christian theologian. As Berger says:

> *Neo-orthodoxy is the reaffirmation of the objective authority of a religious tradition after a period during which that authority had been relativised and weakened.*[3]

As we have seen, this squares with Barth's refusal to allow criteria other than the given Word of God any place in determining Christian theological truth. Faith, he contended, could not be mediated by any human action or experience, and there is no 'human' method by which faith could be attained. However, one of Berger's insights is to demonstrate that, against Barth himself, a method can be discerned. This stems ultimately from Kierkegaard, who was a great influence on Barth in his early thought, and is termed the 'leap of faith'. In a bid to rescue himself from despair and doubt the individual is willing to subject himself to the authority of a tradition which claims immunity from relativization, in a God-given authority. In other words, the decision to 'believe again' is the result of an effort of the will. We discussed the theological problems associated with this 'leaping' in the chapter on exclusivism. Berger's value is that he has uncovered the subjective roots in a sociological analysis of the decision to 'leap' into faith, after a period in which the certainty and plausibility that once supported faith have been radically questioned. The implications of this for Barth's method is that it has no answer to the question 'in which direction should one leap, into which faith?' At the point of crucial importance in the pluralistic world of modernity Barth has no answer to offer. It is not surprising, therefore, that he developed no real theology of religions.

Berger's rejection of exclusivism as the least adequate answer to the questions raised by the 'heretical imperative' led him to place himself firmly in the liberal Protestant tradition, which looks to Schleiermacher as its founder, and which seeks a more 'deliberate reflection about the character and evidential status of religious experience'. In the Christian theology of religions this leads to the pluralist conclusion. But in the light of Berger's analysis what can be said of the intermediary theory of inclusivism? This was not considered by Berger himself, for his concern was primarily with representatives of the Protestant tradition, and those who advocate inclusivism belong mainly in the Catholic Church. Yet we may conjecture that the 'heretical imperative' is given only half an answer by the inclusivists. For on the one hand they assent to the belief that non-Christian faiths also mediate salvation. On the other hand this is qualified by the assertion that the salvation realized there is incomplete, because Christ is not recognized as saviour. What Berger says of nihilation[4] – the means whereby one religious tradition neutralizes the implicit threat by another tradition to its own truth-claims – applies here. The nihilation, for example, practised by Advaita Hinduism towards other religious traditions, which renders them inferior ways and apprehensions of religious truth in comparison with the monist Hindu way, could be viewed as comparable with the inclusivist claims of some Christians. Though Berger himself does not make this comparison, that is no reason for our not making it. Ultimately, inclusivism rests on the foundation which accepts that one revelation at least is free from the relativizations of historical thought. This is in opposition to the 'heretical imperative' and fails to answer fully the questions which are posed by these conditions.

The application of sociological insights and methods to theological problems is illuminating, but cannot be wholly determinative in the vexed question of truth in religion. Sociologists, historians, phenomenologists may be able to map the basic religious alternatives at the level of religious experience, but thereafter the question of a normative standard which transcends the comparison between the different forms of religious expression belongs within the domain of the theologian. If pluralism in the Christian theology of religions meets the challenge of Berger's 'heretical imperative', this does not resolve the remaining problems of the conflicting truth-claims between the faiths. Even in the wider ecumenism proposed by the pluralist theory, the problem of cognitive dissonance has a habit of refusing to give up the ghost. It is necessary to repeat: I have not accepted the view that all faiths are equally true, or of equal value, or are ultimately saying the same thing. Hick's 'Copernician Revolution', Tillich's search for the 'Religion of the

Concrete Spirit' and Cantwell Smith's 'World Theology' do not wish to diminish the very real cognitive clashes which are manifest in the encounter between the faiths. What they do wish to establish is that the divergencies between beliefs are comprehended least by the model which views the truth of one expression as automatically entailing the falsity of another which is at odds with it. Truth, especially in religious matters, belongs within a whole context of life and culture. To say that the divine is manifest in different ways in different cultures is not to side-step the issue of truth in a religiously diverse world, but is to pave the way for a dialogue in which the cognitive discrepancies can be better evaluated in a wider setting. Cantwell Smith summarizes this point well:

> To perceive oneself as in principle heir to the whole religious history of the race thus far, and the community of which one is a member as in principle the human community . . . is not to dissolve the question of religious truth but for our day to bring it into focus.[5]

To believe otherwise, it seems to me, in an age of historical 'en-lightenment' would be an indefensible pre-judgment of truth. Moreover, the Christian may assent to this way of formulating the problem, for the knowledge that God saves everywhere is integral to his Christian faith in the God of history. Accordingly, if 'all human history is Heilsgeschichte',[6] the pluralist theory willingly suspends the *a priori* application of criteria from the specifically Christian heritage in the search to distinguish the more from the less profound, the more from the less 'true' religious belief, and looks to dialogue as the first step on the road to religious truth viewed from a world perspective.

Dialogue, in the truth-seeking sense advocated, has as yet hardly begun. Yet it has begun. Those who remain cautious about its value or direction often include among their reasons a fear of the dissolution of particularity in favour of some all-embracing deadening religious generality, with the consequent loss of religious vitality. These fears are not misplaced, for religions thrive on the particular. Let us examine this relationship between dialogue and religious truth-claims further.

J. J. Lipner has sharpened this issue by drawing attention to two kinds of approach in dialogue. The first he labels 'reduction dialogue', where the participants 'demythologize' the factual content of the claims inherent in religious belief. He cites, as an example, the view which does not attach any factual content to the traditional Christian claim that 'Jesus is the Son of God' but simply responds to it as 'highly subjectivized' poetry. The second approach he labels 'committal dialogue', where participants retain an element of factual content as part of their respective particular beliefs. Not that every traditional factual claim needs to be regarded as sacrosanct, believes Lipner, but sufficient for the dialogue to result in some unresolved conflict, where one claim is not easily assimilated to another. Lipner himself prefers this second approach: 'Where truth-claims conflict, sharpening the focus of their factual content (and this is usually found to be a narrowing down of hitherto larger and confused areas of difference) makes for much progress in unitive understanding.'[7] Now it is part of any dialogue that it should make clear both the differences between the religious traditions and the unity of the divine reality to which they point, the diverse witness and the shared common ground. Does the polarization of 'reduction dialogue' versus 'committal dialogue' aid our holding together these two convictions?

I suggest that Lipner has over-emphasized the incompatibility of the two approaches. On the one hand, he is right to criticize 'reduction dialogue' as long as this implies 'mere subjectivism' in the claim to religious truth, that there is nothing real beyond the personal disposition of the believer which cannot be shared by others. The real opponent of Lipner here is the view of D. Z. Phillips,[8] who holds that religious beliefs are no more than 'pictures' in the mind which regulate one's life, incapable of verification in any sense. The view of religious truth employed in the 'reduction dialogue', believes Lipner, bears a remarkable similarity to Phillips' view. On the other hand, the problem with 'committal dialogue' is that one wonders whether it is ever possible to progress beyond the expressed differences. Elsewhere Lipner says that the Christian faith needs the other faiths in order to 'render more and more "whole" the Christian vision', and that this is possible through dialogue . . . beyond the narrowing incrustations of cultural fetters'.[9] If there is no real meeting between the faiths in 'reduction dialogue' because the factual content of belief has been emptied and the religious claims being made are subjectively limited to particular cultural traditions, then that is not resolved by 'committal dialogue', because here there is no way of telling whether the factual claims are no more than the cultural expressions of one way of faith, and are therefore equally limited. The conflicting truth-claims arise in the first place, as Lipner rightly says, in connection with the revelatory aspects of a religion. For what happens is that realities of this world – persons, events, scriptures – become identified with the transcendent world, in the process of acting as mediators between the two worlds. The problem for theology and inter-religious dialogue is to know how to evaluate the nature of these identifications. What is required in these circumstances is an analysis of religious language which respects Tillich's dictum that 'faith, if it takes its symbols literally becomes idolatrous',[10] and simultaneously does not lapse into vacuity associated with 'mere symbolism'.

The polarization which Lipner has outlined is analogous to what are proposed as alternatives in the debate on the Incarnation. Jesus was either of one substance with the Father (fact-assertive for the purposes of 'committal dialogue'), or Jesus was merely an inspired man (de-mythologized for the purposes of 'reduction dialogue'). In my account of the incarnation I tried to show how it is possible to transcend this division by viewing Jesus as paradigmatic for man's relationship with God. Jesus gave shape to God's purposes and activity at work everywhere in the creation, and to man's response to the divine will. He is significant for the vision of reality which he initiated and for his continuing power to lead others to the same vision in different historical settings. It involved viewing the sonship of Jesus metaphorically, not metaphysically. But this was more than *mere* metaphor. 'Only those who regard directly descriptive language as adequate language,' says Schillebeeckx, 'and thus regard it as the criterion for all language will talk of "*just*" symbolic language.'[11] The style of relationship with God which Jesus initiated represents a genuine encounter with the divine, capable of extending beyond the confines of its cultural origins. The genuineness of the encounter cannot be demonstrated by rational means, but can be verified only in terms of the extent to which it enables those who live in its wake to live according to the vision of life which it yields. Thereafter any verification will be eschatological. Lipner himself also views some form of eschatological verification as the most appropriate method of verification for religious truth-claims.

If this sketch of revelation is valid for the Christian faith, and represents a genuine account of the person of Christ which is symbolic and yet more than merely symbolic, the question arises if a similar account of revelation can function appropriately for other faiths. Peter Slater has made some helpful observations on the functioning of language in religious propositions, which support the view I have been trying to propose:

> The implication of the term 'disclosure' is that there is something previously there to be disclosed . . . But a non-reductive account of metaphors gives them a more dynamic role than this in structuring the realities of meaningful life . . . The element of creativity in our use of symbols makes our situation more open to novelty and change than traditional doctrines of analogy and talk of disclosure have allowed.[12]

Viewing religious language in this way, where symbols possess the quality not only of disclosing reality but also of 'structuring the realities of meaningful life', could be of enormous value in dialogue. Participants could hold on to the differences of religious vision and soteriology which spring partly from the language itself as this has developed in different cultural settings, and yet realize that the transcendent reality which is disclosed through the language is ultimately one.[13] Religious beliefs would function in a way resembling Phillips' picture theory, but go beyond it in claiming some cognitive content for the language, ultimately verified eschatologically. I would agree with Cantwell Smith:

> The task of attaining an epistemological sophistication that will be historically self-critical as well as universalist, is interlinked with, not prior to, our task of attaining corporate critical self-consciousness in the religious realm.[14]

This being the case, there is no reason to fear Phillips' potentially reductive account of religious language. Equally, it means that the dialogue between faiths has much work to do in clarifying the differences and unity in religious experience and belief proposed by the pluralist theory. The intention of dialogue is not therefore to promote generality over particularity. But my contention is that we have reached a point in history when it is no longer permissible to remain comfortable in particularity and to ignore the forces – intellectual, theological, technological – which call for positive relations between the different world faiths. Pluralism in the Christian theology of religions seeks to draw the faiths of the world's religious past into a mutual recognition of one another's truths and values, in order for truth itself to come into proper focus. There are, moreover, good theological reasons why the Christian should not fear this mutual recognition, but should seek it as an expression of Christian truth itself. Some words of Paul Tillich sum up why this is possible, and come close to the heart of what I have been attempting to unfold in the Christian theology of religions:

> In the depth of every religion there is a point at which the religion itself loses its importance, and that to which it points breaks through its particularity elevating it to spiritual freedom and with it to a vision of the spiritual presence in other expressions of the ultimate meaning of man's existence.

This is what Christianity must see in the present encounter of the world religions.[15]

7

TEN YEARS LATER:
SURVEYING THE SCENE

The continued vitality of other major religions in the world since the beginnings of the Christian mission has always been a problem for Christian theologians. Perhaps this was inevitable for a faith which began by proclaiming that the world now lived within the short time span of the *final* age of history (as a result of the salvation won by Christ), and which then had to learn that the final age was going to last for some time! These difficulties, first felt in relation to Judaism, were extended to the other religions. When eventually the largely negative theological location of Judaism in the Christian scheme of things came to be shared by other traditions, the parameters of the Christian theology of the world religions were set.

But the world context for the Christian response to other religious traditions has altered radically. The collective impact of critical thinking in theological method, pressures from 'one world' consciousness, and the experience through inter faith dialogue and friendships of the 'transcendent vision and human transformation' in the heart of 'the other', entails that the degree to which the past can determine our responses to religious plurality in the present is bound to have limits. Today's lively multi-faith environment is both a new context for the re-presentation of the Christian message, and also a considerable challenge to Christian faith itself.[1]

The Christian theology of religions in this book has explored the boundaries of the tension between re-presentation and challenge (mission and dialogue) with the use of the three-fold typology: exclusivism, inclusivism, and pluralism. Since its introduction ten years ago, there have been proposals of alternative typologies and suggestions that we jettison structured typologies altogether. While there is not enough space here to survey all that has been written in ten years, it remains my conviction that the adopted typology retains its continuing value as a rough guide through what is developing as a multi-faceted debate.

Defending the typology

A number of objections have been made to the three-fold typology. First, it is said that the history of global religious life is too complex for the Christian responses to be tailored into three neat options. Secondly, some have said that the options are too internally diverse and overlapping for the typology to do justice to the full representation of responses in the field. Thirdly, questions have been raised about whether the typology allows a sufficient role for the *process* of encounter between *people* from the different religious traditions in shaping any proposed Christian theology of religions.

These criticisms raise some valid points, but I believe that the typology can meet the complaints.

In the first place, while phenomenological analysis shows both how diverse religious traditions really are and how the traditions themselves locate their important emphases variously (in practice, belief, community, or ritual), there is nevertheless a recognizable family likeness between the traditions, such that they can be grouped together as alternative *loci* of 'transcendant vision and human transformation' for their respective adherents. The question of how Christians ought to be responding to these alternative *loci* has generated a spread of responses which the typology was designed broadly to cover.

In response to the second criticism, I have maintained that the three types are not to be treated as rigid categories, and that they are capable of sustaining a number of variations. What has happened over a period of ten years is that an increasing number of theologians have added their own nuance to positions which on the whole, I believe, find a corresponding place within the typology. My impression is that the inclusivist outlook has become the most favoured option among mainline writers in the field.[2]

Dissatisfation with the perceived constrictions of the three-fold typology has also led some to develop alternative options.[3] Perhaps the most pertinent has been the classification of David Lochhead in *The Dialogical Imperative* (SCM Press, London 1988). Lochhead arranges the Christian response to plurality within an ideological framework encompassing 'isolation', 'hostility', 'competition', 'partnership', and 'dialogue'. There are some good correctives in Lochhead's analysis for those who conveniently leave out ideological considerations. However, his conviction that 'it is not possible to separate the question of how the Christian community relates to other religious communities from the more general question of how the Christian community relates to the world'[4] seems to me to beg the question of 'transcendent vision and human transformation' that Christians meet in other faith-communities. This becomes clear when we note that Lochhead's systematic outlook follows Karl Barth, who counted the Christian revelation as *sui generis* among the world's religions. However, Lochhead points to Barth's later writings, and applies Barth's expectation of 'secular parables of the kingdom' analogously to the conditions of religious plurality, thereby interpreting him as being potentially open to truth in other religious traditions.[5] This is in interesting contradiction to the usual interpretation placed on Barth, but in the typology I have adopted, it just as easily draws him into the inclusivist band.

The third objection to the three-fold typology draws attention to the key role of the *process* of encounter and dialogue between religious traditions as a significant factor in developing the Christian theology of religions. Again, there is some truth in this objection, whether it is made from a specific base in process theology itself, or from a more general dialogical perspective. In response, it is important to note that most 'schools' in the Christian theology of religions now advocate a process of dialogue with other traditions. But dialogue serves different purposes and is informed by different theologies. Therefore the stress on process should not become its own justification. Though we should not prescribe the outcome of the dialogue between religions, there are theological assumptions which inform the commitment to the process, even if these are also presented provisionally.

Let me illustrate this point with reference to the process

theologian John Cobb, who is committed to the mutual trans-formation of religious traditions as a result of open inter faith encounter. However, this does not mean that Cobb does not bring theological assumptions to the dialogue. He writes from a christo-centric perspective, yet claims that faithfulness to Jesus requires Christians to expand their circle of awareness to include 'wisdom' from other religious traditions. But that circle, he continues, 'does not become simply the sum total of all those histories told in any way and from any perspective. On the contrary, we appropriate all into an enlarging history whose center remains, for us, Jesus. It is the nature of that center to allow and demand the expansion of the circumference.'[6] This reads like a version of inclusivism, though we might wonder whether the 'for us' in relation to the role of Jesus edges him towards a pluralist outlook. In fact, Cobb eschews either label. But he also leaves unclear the precise relationship between his theological assumptions and his commitment to the process of transformation by dialogue. There seems to be more than a faint echo of his previous disposition towards a form of inclusivism which was firmer about the Logos as 'distinctively embodied in Jesus'.[7]

The typology further illustrated

Turning now to the analysis of developments over ten years, I shall explore the issues using my adopted typological headings. I shall cover points where it seems suitable for reasons that I hope will become clear.

1. Exclusivism

Lesslie Newbigin has been one of the most vociferous defenders of the Christian faith as the sole means for offering a focus of hope and faith for the western world, which he perceives as disintegrat-ing spiritually and intellectually. But as the western world and its values have penetrated deeply into most of the rest of the world's cultures, including cultures informed by alternative religious visions, the Christian faith therefore becomes *the* vision for the whole world.

In Chapter 2 I noted how Newbigin accepted the basic Kraemerian distinction, derived from Karl Barth, between 'religion' and 'revelation', the former being interpreted as the product of human devising and the latter as stemming from the divine initiative. But Kraemer's exclusivist stance *vis-à-vis* other religious visions, Newbigin contends, sprang primarily from his missionary intention to disentangle the Christian message from its captivity to western culture. While this point may not have been fully appreciated by most commentators on his theology of religions, it sharpens the following issue: does the bid to disentangle the Christian message from European cultural values necessarily entail the negative judgment that Newbigin makes on other religious visions?

In his recent writings, and through the channels of the British-based 'Gospel and Our Culture' movement, Newbigin has sought to underpin his Kraemerian exclusivism, paradoxically, by borrowing from developments in postmodern analysis. Relying on the work of Alasdair MacIntyre,[8] Newbigin is encouraged by the current attack on Enlightenment reason, which had previously been considered by many to be the absolute arbiter of truth in the modern world. Our world is in fact characterized, runs this critique, by a number of 'traditions of rationality', some secular and some religious. It is an illusion to think that there can be an unconditioned or supra-rationality which judges all other forms of rationality. To own up to this state of affairs liberates the Christian 'tradition of rationality', as Newbigin sees it, from the cultural captivity to European Enlightenment cultural values of which he is so suspicious.

With the relativizing of the Enlightenment relativizers, there can be no doubt that a space has been provided for religous belief to regain a measure of self-confidence. But this gain is in relation to secular ideology in so far as the latter has tried to eclipse the reality of God by the appeal to the constraints of reason alone. Newbigin goes further than this, however, by seizing an opportunity to reassert Christian exclusivism: 'To affirm the unique decisiveness of God's action in Jesus Christ is not arrogance; it is the enduring bulwark against the arrogance of every culture to be itself the criterion by which others are judged. The charge of arrogance which is levelled against those who speak of Jesus as unique Lord and Saviour must be thrown back at those who assume that "modern historical consciousness" has disposed of that faith.'[9] This strikes me as exaggerated a claim as the rigid view of the impact of the Enlightenment he seeks to dethrone.

It may be unwarranted to claim, as some versions of Enlightenment reason have done, that modern historical consciousness logically entails the relativizing of all 'traditions of rationality' such that history can never be the locus for an 'absolute personality' or an 'absolute religion'. But what surely cannot be ignored is the *deep enmeshment* between the rise of a religious tradition and the cultural forces that have shaped it. Consequently, there can be no access to Christian truth apart from the role played by the processes of interpretation and critical reasoning that have become so much part of theological accountability today. If this is correct, then the form of the cultural *independence* of the Christian revelation so necessary for Newbigin's exclusivist case seems well-nigh impossible to establish.

Newbigin is aware that cultural conditioning has shaped the Christian 'tradition of rationality', and he seeks to give further reasons why the Christian revelation ought to be accepted as the one and only revelation that the world needs. These consist of claims that Christian faith is more significant than other religions because it takes its rise from real historical events in history. In particular, Newbigin points to the traditional understanding of the atonement rooted in the event of the cross: 'Here, where the incarnate Lord suffered and died for the sin of the world, is the *one* (italics mine) place where humankind can truly find its unity, for it is the 'mercy-seat' where sin is forgiven and where, therefore, we can learn to forgive one another.'[10]

Again, I think that Newbigin has overplayed his hand. Not only is the reality of forgiveness prevalent within other religious traditions, but also traditional atonement theory is not the only understanding of the cross available in the Christian tradition. The Christian story of the cross can speak of the love of God in a particularly poignant manner, but it need not be interpreted in an exclusivist direction. When Newbigin says that the cross is the '*one* place where humankind can truly find its unity', this seems to me to by-pass too conveniently the soteriological centres of the other world religions in an age which has learned of the conditioned particularity of all belief and experience.

Newbigin's case for exclusivism remains arbitrary. To rescue the transcendent heart of Christian faith from the inflated claims of certain western (secular) 'traditions of rationality' is reasonable apologetics; to think that this displaces the transcendent heart of other religious traditions is unreasonable dogmatics.

2. Inclusivism

The inclusivist interpretation is usually proffered on the grounds that it represents a kind of via media between the other two options. So: 'Rahner's inclusivist paradigm', writes Gavin D'Costa, 'provides a satisfactory reconciliation of the strengths of the pluralist and exclusivist paradigms while overcoming their shortcomings and weaknesses.'[11] The positive aspects of exclusivism and pluralism, respectively, are that the former retains the normative value of the Christian message for the whole world, and the latter accepts the positive value of the world religions as distinctive 'contexts of salvation'. The weaknesses are that exclusivism represents an unnecessary narrowing of the implications of central Christian beliefs, and that pluralism seems to abandon the normative value of Christian truth-claims as criteria for distinguishing between religious belief and practices.

The main problem for the inclusivist is whether the tension between the absoluteness of Christ as universal saviour can be reconciled with the affirmation of the 'salvific' presence of God throughout creation. Two moves in traditional Christian doctrine, one focussing on Christ and the other on the Spirit, have been explored in recent years in a bid to resolve this tension.

In the first place, attention has shifted from speaking of Christ as *absolute* or *unique*, to using terms such as *normative* or *decisive*, which carry a less *a priori* judgmental overtone. (All of these words are of course capable of multiple interpretations, but the shift here is clear enough.) But it does not remove the basic difficulty. First, it retains the strange doctrine that the salvation won through Jesus has been operative centuries before his historical existence. And, secondly, the tension between the universal 'salvific' presence of God in creation and the traditional notion that Christ must be unsurpassable/final (*normative*, *decisive*) has been convincingly shown to be an intolerable conflict, given an evolutionary-historical understanding of the universe. As Maurice Wiles writes: 'A broadly evolutionary understanding certainly allows room for the emergence of the genuinely new, a *metabasis eis allo genos* of the kind Rahner understands the incarnation to be. But it does not seem able to allow for that new emergent to be final and unrepeatable, which is also for Rahner a part of the understanding of the incarnation.'[12] In other words, at this point, exclusivist and inclusivist understandings look like two sides of the same coin, in so far as neither are fully able to absorb the real implications of historical consciousness.

Inclusivists, aware of the *a priori* judgment on other religions, also offer two further points in order to ameliorate the effects of their position. So D'Costa, for example, points out how orthodox christology in the context of the Christian theology of religions requires to be supplemented, first, by some evidence from the history of religions that Christ does indeed 'include' goodness and truth as glimpsed through other traditions; and, second, by a recognition that other traditions may in some respects 'deepen' or even 'correct' the Christian faith.[13] What is to be said on these scores?

It seems to me to be an extremely difficult hermeneutical and historical task to demonstrate how other religious traditions are historically oriented towards Christ. This has been, of course, the standard judgment of Christianity over against Judaism; but many theologians think this view is untenable in the light of history itself. If it has been abandoned in relation to Judaism, where it functioned primarily as part of the nexus between the parent Judaism and the Christian off-spring, it is strange to want to reinstate it in relation to other religions. On D'Costa's second point, it is a mark of humility to be applauded that a religious tradition should assent to being 'deepened' or 'corrected' by others. However, we are left wondering whether, with this information, the reason for the existence of other religions is in order only to serve Christ and the Christian faith!

The other route suggested for resolving the inclusivist's dilemmas lies in emphasizing the work of the Spirit. Let me take as an example the ecumenical 1990 Baar (Switzerland) Statement, which was prepared for the World Council of Churches Assembly in Canberra the following year.[14] A key sentence is the following: 'We affirm that God has been present in their (the plurality of religious traditions) seeking and *finding* (my italics), that where there is truth and wisdom in their teachings, and love and holiness in their living, this like any wisdom, insight, knowledge, understanding, love and holiness that is found among us is the gift of the Holy Spirit.' In the language of the orthodox trinitarian framework adopted by the Statement, this places a greater emphasis on the independent role of the Spirit in creation, and therefore a greater possibility that other religious traditions can be accepted as distinctively different and not necessarily *a priori* oriented on Christ.

However, the tension involved in the inclusivist position is not wholly resolved within the orthodox trinitarian framework, for the Spirit is also the Spirit of Christ. Therefore the Statement continues: 'We affirm that in Jesus Christ, the incarnate Word, the entire human family has been united to God in an irrevocable bond and covenant. The saving presence of God's activity in all creation and human history comes to the focal point in the event of Christ.' It seems to me that there is no escape from this difficulty of pre-judging the supremacy of Christ within this orthodox framework.

It is possible that I have been over-hasty in my own judgment at this point. Paul Knitter, for example, is convinced that a strong emphasis (stronger than in the Statement itself) on the independence of the work of the Spirit prevents the Christian from 'including' the truth of the other traditions into Christianity. With the radical independence of the Spirit, the relationship between the Spirit and the Word (Christ) becomes one of necessary *relatedness*, not subordination. But there is more. In Knitter's words: 'Perhaps there is a real analogy between the way we might describe the religions and the way scholastic theology has described the persons of the Trinity: they are *relationes susistentes* – subsistent relations, subsisting as really different entities, but living out or realizing their differences in relationship to each other. The most appropriate model for a theology of religions is not one of inclusivism or pluralism, but one of relationality.' A similar suggestion has been made by Michael Barnes: 'The interfaith dialogue actually mirrors the life of the Trinity.'[15]

While the doctrine of the Trinity (the 'social' view of the Trinity, in these discussions) is enjoying something of a revival among the more orthodox Christian theologians, it also remains highly problematic in its own terms. Therefore it is difficult to know exactly what to make of the appeal to Trinitarian doctrine in the context of theology of religions. If it is being used as an illustration of how the Many (the religions) and the One (ultimate reality) could be related, then its usefulness depends only on its illustrative power. But it is hard to know how the Trinity could function as an illustration of anything, given the fact that it is itself a contested, changing and unsettled construct.

What of the suggestion, however, that the Trinity is the best analogy for describing the relationship between the religions on the assumption that the nature of ultimate reality itself is trinitarian? The problem with this is that the Trinity itself is based on an analogy; and so we would be applying one analogous understanding as the basis for another. Moreover, at the heart of the analogy of the 'social' Trinity itself there is a deep epistemological difficulty. It is well known that the doctrine of the 'social' Trinity cannot rest on the functional basis of Father as Creator, Son as Redeemer, and Spirit as Sanctifier. For, in orthodox terms, all three persons of the Trinity are said to act in concert in the world; and the differences between the 'persons' are therefore internal to the life of the Godhead. But the application of the analogy of the Trinity in the pneumatological theology of religions is being made on the grounds that adjustments in the *functional* operations of the Trinity – granting greater indepen- dence to the work of the Spirit – can suffice for the application itself to be valid. This whole approach, the more the problematic nature of the doctrine of the Trinity itself is grasped, seems strangely contrived.

3. Pluralism

During ten years, the pluralist outlook has both expanded and also come under intense criticism. The expansion is best illustrated by John Hick and Paul Knitter (eds), *The Myth of Christian Uniqueness* (SCM Press, London/Orbis Books, Maryknoll 1987), and the criticisms by Gavin D'Costa (ed.), *Christian Uniqueness Reconsidered* (Orbis Books, Maryknoll 1990). At the risk of over simplification, some of the central points of both volumes can be set out as follows.

The Myth argues on three broad fronts for renouncing

the traditional claims of the absolute uniqueness of Christ and Christianity, and so for 'crossing the theological rubicon' to Pluralism: (1) historical consciousness has relativized all the religious traditions, such that none can reasonably claim absolute uniqueness; (2) it is theologically reasonable to expect that the ineffable mystery of ultimate reality can be approached through more than one contingent form; and (3) the assumption of Christian experience as the norm for others fosters an exploitative relationship which runs counter to the demands of global liberation. The parallel criticisms that have been mounted include the following: (1) historical consciousness does not necessarily entail total relativism, which would reduce the traditions to being merely functions of history; (2) that ultimate reality cannot be fully known through one tradition alone does not mean that all traditions participate in some common core of religious experience, which is what seems to be assumed by the pluralist positions; and (3) the ethical criteria of liberation are as tradition-linked as truth-criteria, and therefore the religions cannot avoid employing their normative criteria in judging between true and false, and good and bad religion.

While I do not have the space here to rehearse all three aspects of the debate in detail, I will nevertheless consider each concern briefly. While the criticisms of the pluralist case perhaps chasten the enthusiasm of the pluralist for an easy solution to the problems of the encounter between traditions, I believe that in principle they can be met.

First, in relation to historical consciousness, I noted earlier (p. 159) that it did not necessarily lead to ideological relativism, of the kind that ruled out *a priori* any notion of an 'absolute personality' or an 'absolute religion' appearing in history. But the impact of historical consciousness on the theology of religions is more penetrating than that. It can be put in the same terms as those expressed by the later Ernst Troeltsch: 'Man's age upon the earth amounts to several hundred thousand years or more. His future may come to still more. It is hard to imagine a single point of history along this line, and that the centre-point of our own religious history, as the sole centre of all humanity. That looks far too much like the absolutizing of our own contingent area of life. That is in religion what geocentricism and anthropocentrism are in cosmology and metaphysics. The whole logic of Christo-centrism places it with these other centrisms.'[16] Together with the observation that the 'contingent areas of life' in tradition and belief are deeply conditioned by cultural factors, this point places the burden of proof on those who wish to retain the absolute uniqueness of Christ.

The second area of debate for the pluralist case has been whether the religions participate in some common core experience which is, in turn, said to take different forms according to historical and cultural circumstances. While this may have been the impression given by some early versions of Pluralism, it is incorrect to think that the pluralist option rests on this assumption. However, recognition that believers in the various traditions experience and characterize ultimate reality according to their own distinctive historico-religious matrix need not leave the religions wholly incommensurable at the epistemological level. For each tradition affirms a distinction – expressed in various linguistic ways in the traditions – between ultimate reality as 'unknown-in-itself' and as 'known-through-worldly-form'. By way of example, this distinction has been applied in Christian-Hindu dialogue by the Indian Christian theologian, Stanley Samartha, who suggests that '"Brahman is *sat-cit-ananda*" and "God is triune, Father, Son, and Holy Spirit" could be regarded as two responses to the same Mystery in two cultural settings.'[17] There is carefulness about the intellectual shape of this position which does not match the caricature of it as a variation of the 'many roads lead to God' of popular (mis)understanding.

The usefulness of the distinction between the hiddenness of ultimate reality and the many characterizations of its experienced forms has been refined over ten years, perhaps most persistently by John Hick.[18] Its advantage is that it takes seriously the distinctive character of the religions, without either accepting a total incommensurability between the religions or affirming the supremacy, overt and covert, of the Christian faith-commitment over other faith-commitments.

Not all commentators sympathetic to the concerns of the pluralist case, however, are convinced by the details of their argument. Objections come from two directions. John Cobb, for example, convinced that Pluralism represents a subtle version of the 'common essence' approach, questions the 'assumption that there is a one-to-one correspondence between what is thought of as "ultimate reality" in our Western tradition and that with which all "religious" traditions concern themselves'.[19] From a different direction, Raimundo Panikkar warns of the incipient imperialism within formulations of pluralism that rely purely on western metaphysics. He explicitly affirms the dialogical plurality of ultimates in what he calls 'concord': 'Concord is neither oneness nor plurality. It is the dynamism of the Many toward the One without ceasing to be different and without becoming one, *and without reaching a higher synthesis* . . . The Christian symbol is the Trinity.'[20] For Panikkar, theories of the ultimate *unity* of the religions do not take the *plurality* of global religious life seriously enough!

How should we interpret these objections to the pluralist hypothesis? In response to the question whether ultimate reality may be plural, we can accept that this has to remain a logical possibility (though the problems with applying the doctrine of the Trinity have been mentioned above). However, from the religious point of view, there is one factor which tells against this hypothesis, and that is that the traditions themselves severally affirm ultimate reality as a unity – as the creative ground of all things, or as the true nature of life itself. Again, it could be the case that, given a radically new phase in global historical life beyond what the traditions could ever have envisaged, the plurality of ultimates has to remain a possibility. But it is interesting that both Cobb and Panikkar, who in their different ways want to retain a strong sense of continuity with the Christian tradition, are nevertheless prepared to entertain what the Christian tradition has never sanctioned! On the other hand, the hypothesis of pluralism provides, in John Hick's words, 'the simplest way of accounting for the data.'[21] In this respect, the adjustment of accepting the validity of other religious traditions, entailed by pluralism, seems less of a severance from tradition than does the acceptance of a possible plurality of ultimates.

The third problematic area for the pluralist case, in recent years, concerns the criteria by which we are to judge religious responses to life. Clearly there must be some limits to what is acceptable in religious expression, for it is notorious to the extent to which religious commitment is open to abuse. In the pluralist case the problems are heightened for obvious reasons. Does it mean that without the application of criteria from one tradition alone the pluralist is standing in a kind of meta-position, claiming an overview which itself is probably a form of covert Christian imperialism?

There are two comments to make. First, the pluralist position is constructed *inductively*, that is to say it accepts that other religious 'ways' are *loci* of transcendent vision and human transformation. Of course, there is no way of knowing, from Christian criteria alone, that these *loci* are in fact 'salvific' in the ways that they claim – except, that is, in the manner which uses those criteria as a measuring apparatus for the status of others. Rejecting this practice, however, we are left to trust that other traditions are 'salvation-bearing'. But it is an act of trust which is also built on the experience of others and on what we know through their scriptures and traditions. We apply the same rules of 'informed trust' towards other traditions as we assume in the Christian experience of the religious response to life. This is not so much a meta-position as a tradition-position which has opened itself sideways, as it were, to accept the validity of the other.

Therefore it is incorrect of Gavin D'Costa, for example, to claim that 'A recognition of God's universal action cannot proceed without a normative Christology.'[22] Christ is normative for Christians and universally significant for the world. But there are other instances and sources where the love of God has been embodied, and there is no evidence to suggest that these 'revelations' are inferior to the Christian instance. Further, it is untrue to suggest that pluralists have surrendered their focus on Jesus altogether. The question is what view of Jesus is appropriate for today. I see no reason to change my mind in general terms from what I have written about christology in Chapter 5. In relation to other religions, Jesus remains normative for Christians, generating a faith of 'universal intention and destiny' to be exercised openly in dialogue.[23] I have written elsewhere of how the traditional doctrine of the Incarnation has become increasingly either arbitrary or ambiguous in the context of our multi-faith environment.[24]

Expressing similar anxieties about the loss of normative criteria in judging the truth of the religions, Hans Küng has also criticized the pluralist position. In wanting to transcend the three-fold typology, he advocates his own form of open dialogue between the traditions based on ethical considerations. But Küng's own balancing act between what he knows to be true of other traditions and what he counts as normative Christian conviction is unconvincing. He simply *observes* two perspectives:

> Seen from outside . . . there are of course true religions . . . There are different ways of salvation (with different saving figures) towards the one goal, which can even partly overlap and which at all events can mutually fructify one another.

And:

> Seen from the inside . . . there is only one true religion: Christianity . . . However, the one true religion in no way excludes truth in other religions, but can allow their validity: with qualifications they are true religions (in this sense 'conditioned' or in some way 'true').[25]

This draws Küng into the inclusivist position of his earlier *On Being a Christian* (see pp. 62–64), in spite of the best intentions of his whole developing outlook. An open dialogue between 'true' partners ('outside perspective') on the basis that Christian faith retains the final and normative criteria of truth ('inside perspective') is a contradiction in terms.

The second point about criteria in relation to the pluralist case is that the traditions use overlapping common criteria, derived from the ethical dimension within religious commitment. At the general level these are compassion, love, honesty, truthfulness, and so on, and they can be easily summarized under the Golden Rule: 'do to others what you would have then do to you.' In so far as the religions seek to promote the transformation of the self and society to true relationship with ultimate reality, glimpsed through the matrix of different religious patterns of response, the overlapping ethical criteria provide the means for deciding on the boundaries of acceptable and non-acceptable religious belief and practice. One expression of this proposal was taken up by religious leaders at the Centenary of the World's Parliament of Religions in Chicago in 1993 when they affirmed that 'a common set of core values is found in the teachings of the religions, and that these form the basis of a global ethic'.[26]

Clearly there is much work of mutual criticism and self-criticism for adherents from the different traditions to do if the application of these criteria is to move beyond the level of generality characteristic of global ethics. In practice, the traditions have exhibited much cruelty in history, as well as much good. But in so far as the ethics of a tradition are part of its whole outlook, it could be objected that raising up ethical criteria in this manner simply repeats the problem of the incommensurability of religious systems in another form. Keith Ward's recommendation meets this objection to a degree: 'It might be better to see the different faiths, not as in radical opposition but as having a range of agreed values, but varying ways of interpreting them in the light of a developing understanding of the world.'[27] But does this kind of formulation still ride rough-shod over the deep differences between the shape that the religions give to their ethical values? The answer to that question depends upon the extent to which our values are inextricably bound up with answers to questions in religious cosmology and eschatology.

What then of the differing truth-claims between the religions at these levels? Is the world created '*ex nihilo*' or is it an emanation? Are human beings resurrected or reincarnated after death; or neither? Hick's answer to this challenge is to place the question about conflicting truth-claims in an alternative light. Borrowing from the notion of the Buddha's 'unanswered questions', Hick suggests that we do not need to know the answers to the questions about the origins of life, eschatology, and so on, before believers set out on the path of 'salvation'. Therefore we should learn to tolerate differences at these levels.[28]

But again the questions: are 'belief' and 'salvation' more intrinsically linked than the strong separation between the two that the Buddha upholds? Might the appropriation of the strong separation turn out to be a form of misappropriation, that is, one which cannot be accepted by Christians without changing the whole character of Christian faith itself? I think that this would be pressing the objection too strongly. Those Christians who are not convinced by the pluralist argument at this point need to remember that the issue of 'salvation' is not dependent on resolutions to the internal disagreements within the churches about points of doctrine. Disagreements at the propositional level remain, but they are secondary to the experience and practice of 'salvation'. It is this same principle which is being extended to the relationship between the religions.

It is worth recalling that this whole question of conflicting truth-claims may be more of a problem for the Christian tradition than for many others because of its long pedigree of emphasizing correct belief. Nevertheless, it is also worth recalling that we are learning, through the impact of critical thinking, that Christian commitment is not best characterized as a function of the usual division between orthodoxy and heresy. This same principle can, again, apply in the formulation of a Christian theology of religions.

To repeat: the conflicting truth-claims – metaphysical and historical – between the traditions are important in their own terms. Pluralism has not accepted that religious truth-claims are wholly non-factual. But the differences between traditions at these levels have to be argued over in a spirit which recognizes what is at stake – different kinds of disagreements which are open, or partially open, to different kinds of evidence, and which are susceptible to the ethical criterion of the (individual and social) spiritual fruits they promote. Therefore, they need not be the stumbling block to a pluralist theology of religions that they are often taken to represent.

The Christian theology of religions has mostly concentrated on the epistemological questions in the relationship of Christian faith to ultimate reality and to the other religions. This is inevitable given both the Greek conceptual heritage and the challenge of the Enlightenment contesting the basic validity of religious experience itself. For these reasons the discussion between options in a typology can tend towards an air of static rationalism. One of the criticisms of the pluralist position has been that it is perhaps the most prone to appearing to be offering an all-explanatory rational system in this bad sense. If the pluralist position is to attract more support it will need to demonstrate, more clearly than it has to date, how it is inherently a dynamic hypothesis.

Let me therefore end this review of ten years with a very brief sketch of some of the issues that need further exploration in the pluralist option, as a means of drawing out its dynamic sense.

First, there is the need to show in what sense the traditions are complementary. An example of how this might be conceived comes from Aloysius Pieris, who notes from his Sri Lankan context that the 'liberative knowledge' of Buddhism and the 'redemptive love' of Christianity exist in 'indefinable contrast'. 'And yet,' he continues, 'it must be recognized that both gnosis and agape are *necessary* precisely because each in itself is *inadequate* as a medium not only for experiencing but also for expressing our intimate moments with the Ultimate Source of liberation. They are . . . complementary idioms that need each other to mediate the self-transcending experience called "salvation".'[29] This view does not entail that all traditions represent parts of the total truth as pieces of a jig-saw contribute towards the totality of the final picture, but that different traditions view the fullness of religious truth through the partiality of their own single tradition. In this sense the dynamic complementarity exists to counteract the isolation of any one vision of religious truth in relation to ultimate reality.

Secondly, there is a need to supplement overarching theories in the Christian theology of religions with the realities of bi-lateral dialogue. Some of these dialogues have begun to show how some of the oppositional stances between traditions need not be so stark as we used to think. For example, the Jewish–Christian dialogue has begun unravelling some of the deep suspicions between the two communities that have existed since the beginning of the Christian era. So (some) Christians are re-learning the implications of the Jewishness of Jesus, and (some) Jews are creating what Tony Bayfield has called 'theological space' for Christian faith, in spite of the latter's historical anti-Judaism.[30] The examples could be multiplied now. But the impact of these bi-lateral exchanges is that they are able to draw out the similarities and differences between the traditions in the dynamic inter-play of dialogue.

A third need is for religious dialogue to show how the traditions through creative exchange are responding to the great global crises of our day, such as poverty, war, human rights, ecology and so on. This is not simply a question of how the traditions can cooperate in practical ways to bring about change for a better world order. It is also a matter of how the global conditions themselves challenge our visions of ultimate reality, and particularly the tendencies towards fatalism in all the traditions. Both the concept of divine sovereignty in the semitic/prophetic traditions, and the concept of the return to the oneness of all reality in the Indian/mystical traditions can undermine that sense of radical human responsibility so needful for future survival. Dialogue in this context would drive the traditions to more imaginative exchanges at the levels of both belief and ethics.[31]

During the last ten years the issues of the Christian responses to religious plurality have assumed a much greater place on the theological agenda of both the Church and the Academy. In this survey I have reaffirmed many of the points I made ten years ago. This is mainly because I have not found any satisfactory alternatives to the pluralist hypothesis in the intervening period. Many of the objections to it have either been dealing with misrepresentations, or even caricatures. It is also true that the pluralist hypothesis has been refining itself. I trust that this chapter has contributed to that process of refinement.

NOTES

Chapter 1   The Problem

1. W. C. Smith, *The Faith of Other Men*, Harper Torchbooks, New York 1972, p. 133.
2. Cited by Smith, op. cit., p. 121.
3. M. A. C. Warren, from the General Introduction to the 'Christian Presence' Series, SCM Press 1959ff.
4. Paul Tillich, 'The Significance of the History of Religions for the Systematic Theologian', in *The Future of Religions*, Harper & Row, New York/Greenwood Press, London 1966, p. 91.
5. Loc. cit.
6. J. A. Veitch, 'The Case for a Theology of Religions', in *Scottish Journal of Theology*, Vol. 24, No. 4, Nov. 1971, p. 408.

Chapter 2   Exclusivism

1. Cited by Hans Küng in his essay, 'The World Religions in God's Plan of Salvation', in J. Neuner (ed.), *Christian Revelation and World Religions*, Burns and Oates, London 1967, p. 26.
2. Hendrik Kraemer, *The Christian Message in a Non-Christian World*, The Edinburgh House Press, London 1938, p. 106.
3. Karl Barth, *Church Dogmatics*, Vol. 1/2, T. & T. Clark, Edinburgh 1956, p. 302.
4. Ibid., p. 309.
5. Ibid., p. 295.
6. Ibid., p. 327.
7. Ibid., p. 301.
8. Karl Barth, *Church Dogmatics*, Vol. 4/3, T. & T. Clark, Edinburgh 1962, p. 575.
9. Ibid., p. 810.
10. J. A. Veitch, 'Revelation and Religion in the Theology of Karl Barth', in *Scottish Journal of Theology*, No. 1, Feb. 1971, p. 20.
11. *Church Dogmatics*. Vol. 1/2, p. 296 (parenthesis mine).
12. Cited by Gerald H. Anderson, 'Religion as a Problem for the Christian Mission', in D. Dawe and J. Carmen (eds.), *Christian Faith in a Religiously Plural World*, Orbis Books, Maryknoll, New York 1978, p. 114.
13. C. J. Bleeker, *Christ in Modern Athens*, E. J. Brill, Leiden 1965, pp. 93ff.

14. Hendrik Kraemer, *Religion and the Christian Faith*, Lutterworth Press, London 1956, p. 193.

15. Emil Brunner, *Revelation and Reason*, SCM Press, London/Westminster Press, Philadelphia 1947, p. 270.

16. *The Christian Message*, p. 126.

17. *Revelation and Reason*, p. 262.

18. *Religion and the Christian Faith*, p. 353.

19. Ibid., p. 356.

20. *Revelation and Reason*, p. 270.

21. Ibid., p. 236.

22. Ibid., p. 235.

23. *The Christian Message*, p. ix.

24. Hendrik Kraemer, *Why Christianity of All Religions?*, Lutterworth Press, London 1962, p. 79.

25. Ibid., p. 93.

26. Ibid., p. 99.

27. W. C. Smith, *The Faith of Other Men*, Harper Torchbooks, New York 1972, p. 134.

28. Küng, art. cit., p. 31.

29. Cited by Küng, pp. 32f.

30. Lesslie Newbigin, *The Open Secret*, Eerdmans, Michigan 1978, p. 198. See also his *Christian Witness in a Plural Society*, BCC 1977, p. 10.

31. *Christian Witness*, p. 9.

32. *The Open Secret*, p. 205. See also his article 'Interfaith Dialogue', *Scottish Journal of Theology*, Vol. 30, No. 3, June 1977, which repeats some of the paragraphs in *The Christian Witness* and *The Open Secret*.

33. D. F. Ford, 'Conclusion: Assessing Barth', in S. W. Sykes (ed.), *Karl Barth – Studies of his Theological Method*, Clarendon Press, Oxford 1979, p. 195.

34. A. K. Cragg, *The Christian and Other Religion*, Mowbrays, London and Oxford 1977, p. 71.

35. *The Christian Message*, p. 65.

36. *Why Christianity of All Religions?*, p. 72.

37. Ibid., p. 117.

38. Ibid., p. 83.

39. Lesslie Newbigin, 'The Centrality of Jesus for History', in M. Goulder (ed.), *Incarnation and Myth*, SCM Press, London 1979, p. 206.

40. *Christian Witness*, p. 15.

Chapter 3   Inclusivism

1. Hans Küng, 'The World Religions in God's Plan of Salvation' in Joseph Neuner (ed.), *Christian Revelation and World Religions*, Burns and Oates, London 1967, p. 27.

2. See for example John Drury, *Tradition and Design in Luke's Gospel*, Darton, Longman & Todd, London 1976, ch. 2.

Notes

3. 1 *Apology* 46, 1–4.
4. Austin Flannery, OP (ed.), *Vatican Council II. The Conciliar and Post-Conciliar Documents*, Dominican Publications, St Saviour's, Dublin, Ireland 1975, p. 739.
5. Ibid., p. 738.
6. Ibid., p. 739.
7. Ibid., p. 367f.
8. Ibid., p. 814.
9. See his essay 'The World Religions in God's Plan of Salvation'.
10. Karl Rahner, *Theological Investigations*, Vol. 5, Darton, Longman & Todd, London 1966, p. 118.
11. Ibid., p. 121.
12. Karl Rahner, *Theological Investigations*, Vol. 6, Darton, Longman & Todd, London 1969, p. 393.
13. Ibid., p. 392.
14. Ibid., p. 394.
15. Rahner, Vol. 5, p. 131. Rahner sometimes uses the term 'anonymous Christianity', though he is more sure of the term 'anonymous Christian'. In his later writing he recognizes a possible terminological difficulty with 'anonymous Christianity': 'If we are unwilling to go on from this, and to speak of an anonymous *Christianity*, then I will raise no protest against this refusal. All that is involved here is simply a question of what constitutes the terminology that best suits the purpose and so a question of judgement on which I have no fixed opinion whatever. Admittedly I do regard the term "anonymous Christian" as inescapable as long as no one suggests a better term to me' (Vol. 14, 1976, p. 292). Also in his essay, 'Christ in Non-Christian Religions', in G. Gispert-Sauch (ed.), *God's Word among Men*, Vidyajoti, Delhi 1973, he notes in a footnote (p. 97) that the notion of a positive role assigned to religions (as opposed to non-Christian individuals) in mediating salvation is in conflict with Vatican II statements. However, we may say that the Council documents are ambiguous at this point.
16. Raymond Panikkar, *The Unknown Christ of Hinduism*, Darton, Longman & Todd, London 1964, p. 54.
17. Rahner, Vol. 5, p. 133.
18. Rahner, Vol. 6, p. 391.
19. Eugene Hillman, *The Wider Ecumenism: Anonymous Christianity and the Church*, Burns & Oates, London/Herder & Herder, New York 1968, p. 109.
20. Küng, art. cit., p. 64 (parenthesis mine).
21. Ibid., pp. 65f.
22. Metropolitan Georges Khodr, 'Christianity in a Pluralistic World', in *Sobornost*, The Journal of the Fellowship of St Alban and St Sergius, Series 6, No. 3. Summer 1971, p. 171.
23. Ibid., p. 173.
24. H. R. Schlette, *Towards a Theology of Religions*, Burns & Oates, London 1966, p. 78.

25. Ibid., p. 90.

26. Hans Küng, op. cit., p. 52.

27. Cited by James Dupuis SJ, 'The Salvific Value of Non-Christian Religions', in J. Pathrapankal (ed.), *Service and Salvation*, Theological Publications of India, Bangalore 1973, p. 211.

28. Ibid., p. 228.

29. Ibid., p. 229.

30. John Drury, *Tradition and Design in Luke's Gospel*, Darton, Longman and Todd, London 1976, p. 9.

31. M. F. Wiles, *Explorations in Theology 4*, SCM Press, London 1979, p. 32.

32. Anita Röper, *The Anonymous Christian*, Sheed and Ward, London 1966.

33. Cited by E. C. Dewick, *The Gospel and Other Faiths*, The Canterbury Press, London and Edinburgh 1948, p. 96.

34. Op. cit. p. 29.

35. Thomas Merton, 'Contemplation and the Dialogue Between Religions', in *Sobornost*, The Journal of the Fellowship of St Alban and St Sergius, Series 5, No. 8, Winter–Spring 1969, p. 563.

36. Bede Griffiths, *Return to the Centre*, Collins, London 1976, p. 107.

37. Bede Griffiths, *Vedanta and Christian Faith*, The Dawn Horse Press, Los Angeles 1973, p. viii.

38. Bede Griffiths, *Christian Ashram*, Darton, Longman and Todd, London 1966, p. 92.

39. Ibid., p. 81.

40. *Vedanta and Christian Faith*, p. 84.

41. *Return to the Centre*, p. 70.

42. Abhishiktananda, *Saccidananda*, ISPCK, Delhi 1974, p. 194.

43. Hans Küng, *On Being a Christian*, Collins Fount, London 1978, p. 98.

44. Ibid., pp. 113f.

45. J. A. T. Robinson, *Truth is Two-Eyed*, SCM Press, London 1979, p. 98.

46. Ibid., pp. 52f.

47. Ibid., p. 53f.

48. Ibid., p. 54.

49. Ibid., p. 56.

50. Ibid., p. 119.

51. Ibid., p. 117.

52. Ibid., p. 129.

53. Ibid., p. 125.

54. *On Being a Christian*, p. 112.

Chapter 4 Pluralism

1. W. C. Smith, *The Faith of Other Men*, Harper Torchbooks, New York 1972, p. 138. This essay has been reprinted in W. G. Oxtoby (ed.),

Notes

Religious Diversity: Essays by Wilfred Cantwell Smith, Harper and Row, New York 1976; and in J. Hick and B. Hebblethwaite (eds), *Christianity and Other Religions*, Collins Fontana, London 1980. Hereinafter this book is referred to as Hick and Hebblethwaite.

2. The phrase is A. K. Cragg's, in *The Christian and Other Religion*, Mowbrays, London 1977, p. 10.

3. Cited by P. Tillich, *Christianity and the Encounter of the World Religions*, Columbia University Press, New York and London 1963, p. 40f.

4. W. E. Hocking, *Re-Thinking Missions*, Harper and Row, New York 1932, p. 327.

5. Ibid., p. 47.

6. A. Toynbee, *Christianity Among the Religions of the World*, Scribner's, New York 1957, p. 111. Also: O. C. Thomas (ed.), *Attitudes Toward Other Religions*, SCM Press, London and Harper and Row, New York 1969, p. 171. Hereinafter this book is referred to as Thomas.

7. Ibid., p. 104.

8. Ibid., pp. 99f.

9. Ibid., p. 110.

10. W. E. Hocking, *Living Religions and a World Faith*, Allen and Unwin, London and Macmillan, New York 1940, p. 21. It is instructive to compare the views of Cantwell Smith writing twenty years later in *The Faith of Other Men*: 'Perhaps the single most important challenge that mankind faces in our day is the need to turn our nascent world society into a world community . . . My own view is that the task of constructing even that minimum degree of world fellowship that will be necessary for man to survive at all is far too great to be accomplished on any other than a religious basis' (pp. 126f.). Smith would not wish to achieve a coalescence of faiths in a world religion in the way Hocking suggests. But he is giving vent to the urgency which the growing 'one world' forces on theology to construct an understanding of religions that will enable them at least to co-operate in working towards a religious basis for this 'one world'.

11. Ibid., p. 198. The core of Hocking's theory has been reprinted in Thomas. The ideas for the 'Way of Reconception' were present in embryo form in the earlier *Re-thinking Missions*, 'Religion becomes potentially universal in range as it becomes aware of its own inner logic' (p. 7), and, 'As Christianity shares this faith with men of all faiths, they become changed into the same substance' (p. 58).

12. Ibid., p. 196.

13. Ibid., p. 199.

14. Ibid., p. 249.

15. Ibid., p. 229.

16. M. F. Wiles, *Explorations in Theology 4*, SCM Press, London 1979, p. 39.

17. Toynbee, op. cit., p. 96.

18. O. C. Thomas, for example, distinguishes three forms of relativism: cultural, epistemological, and teleological (p. 20). His objections to all three are taken up during the course of our discussion.

19. The phrase is that of J. B. Cobb, *Christ in a Pluralistic Age*, Westminster Press, Philadelphia 1975, p. 58.

20. A. O. Dyson, The *Immortality of the Past*, SCM Press, London 1974, p. 30. Dyson cites this phrasing from a primary source of Troeltsch. I am indebted to Dyson (especially chapter II and IV of his book) for what follows here concerning the wider background of Troeltsch's thought.

21. Thomas, p. 76. Also Hick and Hebblethwaite, p. 14. Both books reprint Troeltsch's essay 'The Place of Christianity among the World Religions' (1923), in *Christian Thought*, Meridian, New York/University of London Press 1957.

22. In the eighteenth century Lessing had written: 'If no historical truth can be demonstrated, then nothing can be demonstrated by historical truths.' Cited by A. R. Vidler, 'Historical Objections', in *Objections to Christian Belief*, Constable, London 1963, p. 61.

23. Dyson, p. 34.

24. Ibid., p. 45.

25. E. Troeltsch, *The Absoluteness of Christianity* (1901), SCM Press, London 1972, p. 90. Cf. the comment on p. 86: 'Only the misguided thought habits of rational or supernatural dogmatism surround the word "relative" with all the terrors of the uncertain, the unstable, the purposeless.'

26. Ibid., pp. 111f.

27. E. Troeltsch, 'The Place of Christianity among World Religions' (1923), in Thomas, p. 86.

28. Ibid., p. 84.

29. Ibid., p. 90.

30. Feuerbach, for instance, derided the distinction between 'God as he is in himself and God as he is for me' as a sceptical one, in his book, *The Essence of Christianity*, Harper Torchbooks, New York 1957, p. 17.

31. W. C. Smith, 'Conflicting Truth-Claims: A Rejoinder', in J. Hick (ed.), *Truth and Dialogue*, Sheldon Press, London 1974, p. 157. Hereinafter this book is referred to as *Truth and Dialogue*.

32. Loc. cit.

33. 'The Place of Christianity', in Thomas, p. 89.

34. J. Hick, *God Has Many Names*, Macmillan, London 1980, p. 52.

35. J. Hick, 'The Outcome: Dialogue into Truth', in *Truth and Dialogue*, p. 152.

36. N. Smart, 'Truth and Religions', in *Truth and Dialogue*, p. 50.

37. J. Hick, 'Towards a Philosophy of Religious Pluralism', in *Neue Zeitschrift für Systematische Theologie und Religionsphilosophie* 22.2, 1980, p. 142.

38. D. B. Forrester, 'Professor Hick and the Universe of Faiths', in *Scottish Journal of Theology*, Vol. 29, 1975, p. 69. See also the objections of L. Newbigin, *The Open Secret*, Eerdmans, Michigan 1978, pp. 185–91; and those of J. Lipner, 'Does Copernicus Help?', *Religious Studies*, Vol. 13, No. 2, June 1977, pp. 243–58.

Notes

39. J. Hick, *God and the Universe of Faiths*, Collins Fount, London 1977, p. 172.

40. Loc. cit.

41. D. H. Smith, 'The Church and the Non-Christian Religions: Co-existence and/or Conflict', in *The Modern Churchman*, No. 1, Oct. 1962, New Series, Vol. VI, p. 110f.

42. E. J. Sharpe, 'The Goals of Inter-Religious Dialogue', in *Truth and Dialogue*, pp. 77ff.

43. *Guidelines on Dialogue with People of Living Faiths and Ideologies*, WCC, Geneva 1979, p. 13.

44. Sharpe, op. cit., p. 90.

45. See, for example, the account of the failure of a Hindu-Christian meeting between C. Murray Rogers and Sivendra Prakash, in C. M. Rogers, 'Dialogue Postponed', *Asia Focus*, 1970, pp. 211–19.

46. H. Küng, *On Being a Christian*, Collins Fount, London 1978, p. 112.

47. A. O. Dyson, *The Immortality of the Past*, SCM Press, London 1974, p. 92. Cf. Stanley Samartha: 'Inter-religious dialogue should also stress the need to study fundamental questions in the religious dimension of life. Religions are man's responses to the mystery of existence and quests for meaning in the midst of confusion. World religious organizations should support the long-range study of the deeper questions which today ought to be taken up not just separately by individuals of each religion, but also together in the larger interests of mankind' ('The Progress and Promise of the Inter-Religious Dialogues', *Journal of Ecumenical Studies*, 1972, pp. 473f.). These remarks are similar to the view I suggest when I say that dialogue must take account of the secular critique of religion.

48. P. Tillich, 'The Significance of the History of Religions for the Systematic Theologian', *The Future of Religions*, Harper and Row, New York/Greenwood Press, London 1966, p. 88.

49. For an introduction to Paul's doctrine of the Spirit it is instructive to read Tillich's sermon, 'The Witness of the Spirit to the Spirit', in *The Shaking of the Foundations*, Penguin Books, Harmondsworth 1963, pp. 133ff. Already by 1949 Tillich considered Paul's doctrine to be the essence of Christianity: ' "The Spirit beareth witness with our spirit that we are the children of God." Something new has come, a new reality, a new being, a Spirit distinguished from our spirit, yet able to make itself understood to our spirit, beyond us and yet in us. The whole message of Christianity is contained in this statement' (p. 137).

50. P. Tillich, *Christianity and the Encounter of the World Religions*, Columbia University Press, New York and London 1963, p. 82.

51. Ibid., p. 67.

52. R. C. Zaehner, 'Religious Truth', in *Truth and Dialogue*, p. 18.

53. J. B. Cobb, *Christ in a Pluralistic Age*, Westminster Press, Philadelphia 1975, p. 60.

54. Ibid., p. 57.

55. W. C. Smith, *Towards a World Theology*, Macmillan, London 1980, p. 101.
56. Ibid., p. 20.
57. Ibid., pp. 113f.
58. Ibid., p. 171.
59. W. C. Smith, *The Meaning and End of Religion*, pp. 168f.
60. *Towards a World Theology*, p. 171. .
61. Ibid., p. 94.
62. Ibid., p. 177.
63. Ibid., p. 96.
64. J. V. Taylor, 'The Theological Basis of Interfaith Dialogue', in Hick and Hebblethwaite, p. 232. This article is also printed in *Crucible*, Jan–March 1978.

Chapter 5   Incarnation and the Christian Theology of Religions

1. Brian Hebblethwaite, 'Incarnation – the Essence of Christianity?', *Theology*, Vol. LXXX, March 1977, No. 674, p. 85.
2. Karl Barth, *Church Dogmatics*, Vol. 1/2, T. & T. Clark, Edinburgh 1956, p. 1.
3. Ibid., p. 297.
4. John Bowden, *Karl Barth*, SCM Press, London 1971, p. 112.
5. Norman Pittenger, *Christology Reconsidered*, SCM Press, London 1970, p. 87.
6. Cited from an extract by Karl Rahner in 'Concise Theological Dictionary', Herder-Burns and Oates, London 1965, and reprinted in John Bowden and James Richmond (eds.), *A Reader in Contemporary Theology*, SCM Press, London 1967, p. 64.
7. Brian Hebblethwaite, 'The Uniqueness of the Incarnation', in M. Goulder (ed.), *Incarnation and Myth: The Debate Continued*, SCM Press, London 1979, p. 189. Hereinafter this collection of papers is referred to as *I&M*.
8. Maurice Wiles in *I&M* (pp. 3ff.) points out the range of meaning 'incarnation' is used to cover.
9. This was effectively the position of B. Hebblethwaite in 'Incarnation' – the essence of Christianity', *Theology*, Vol. LXXX, March 1977, No. 674, pp. 85ff. Cf. the reply by John Hick in his letter in *Theology*, Vol. LXXX, May 1977, No. 675, pp. 204ff.
10. D. M. Baillie, *God Was in Christ*, Faber and Faber, London 1956, p. 117.
11. *I&M*, p. 54.
12. Ibid., p. 61.
13. Cited by M. Wiles, 'Myth in Theology', in *The Myth of God Incarnate*, SCM Press, London 1977, p. 150.
14. Ibid., p. 153.
15. H. W. Bartsch (ed.), *Kerygma and Myth*, Vol. 1, ET SPCK, London 1953.

16. G. Lampe, *God as Spirit*, Clarendon Press, Oxford 1977, p. 142.

17. *The Myth of God Incarnate*, p. 161.

18. Ibid., p. 162.

19. J. Knox, *The Humanity and Divinity of Christ*, Cambridge University Press 1967, p. 107.

20. J. A. T. Robinson, *The Roots of a Radical*, SCM Press, London 1980, p. 65.

21. B. Hebblethwaite, 'Incarnation – the Essence of Christianity?', *Theology*, Vol. LXXX, March 1977, No. 674, p. 88. See also his article in *I&M*, 'Incarnation and Atonement: The Moral and Religious Value of the Incarnation', pp. 87ff.

22. K. Ward, 'Incarnation or Inspiration – A False Dichotomy?', *Theology*, Vol. LXXX, July 1977, No. 676, pp. 251ff.

23. Ibid., p. 253.

24. Ibid., p. 254.

25. Cited by D. E. Nineham, *Explorations in Theology* I, SCM Press, London 1977, p. 156.

26. E. Schillebeeckx, *Interim Report*, SCM Press, London 1980, p. 29. See also the essay by J. A. T. Robinson, 'Need Jesus have been Perfect?', in S. W. Sykes and J. P. Clayton (eds.), *Christ, Faith and History*, Cambridge University Press 1972, pp. 39–52.

27. E. Schillebeeckx, *Jesus. An Experiment in Christology*, Collins, London 1979, p. 75.

28. J. L. Houlden, *Patterns of Faith*, SCM Press, London 1977, p. 55.

29. C. F. D. Moule, *The Origin of Christology*, Cambridge University Press 1977, p. 138.

30. J. Knox, op. cit., p. 113.

31. Cited by John Robinson in his *Truth is Two-Eyed*, SCM Press, London 1979, p. 123.

32. N. Pittenger, op. cit., pp. 138f.

33. Ibid., p. 143.

34. E. Schillebeeckx, *Jesus. An Experiment in Christology*, p. 557.

35. Ibid., p. 658.

36. Ibid., p. 669.

37. E. Schillebeeckx, *Christ. The Christian Experience in the Modern World*, p. 48.

38. Ibid., p. 838.

39. E. Schillebeeckx, *Interim Report*, SCM Press, London 1980, p. 142.

40. I do not argue the case here, though I realize that there are some theologians who have recently attempted to make it central to their Christian claims. I agree with Frances Young's comment in her essay, 'The Finality of Christ', in *I&M*: 'In spite of the current interest in eschatology stimulated by the theology of Pannenberg and Moltmann, it is doubtful whether the eschatological version of the claim to Christ's finality, linked as it is to the cultural conditions of the ancient world Jewish and Hellenistic, can now, be revitalized outside rather specialist theological circles' (p. 185).

41. N. Pittenger, 'Christology in Process Theology', *Theology*, Vol. LXXX, May 1977, No. 675, p. 193. Cited by Robinson, pp. 125f.
42. *Truth is Two-Eyed*, p. 121.
43. Ibid., p. 125.
44. Ibid., p. 99.
45. N. Pittenger, *Christology Reconsidered*, pp. 103f.
46. 'Christology in Process Theology', p. 193.
47. J. Hick, 'Jesus and the World Religions', in *The Myth of God Incarnate*, p. 182.
48. See his article, 'The Centrality of Jesus for History', in *I&M*, pp. 197ff.
49. F. Young, 'The Finality of Christ', in *I&M*, p. 185.

Chapter 6   A Question of Truth

1. P. L. Berger, *The Heretical Imperative*, Collins, London 1980, p. 28.
2. Ibid., p. 33.
3. Ibid., p. 79.
4. Ibid., p. 169.
5. W. C. Smith, *Towards a World Theology*, p. 188.
6. Ibid., p. 172.
7. J. Lipner, 'Truth-Claims and Inter-Religious Dialogue', in *Religious Studies*, Vol. 12, 1976, p. 230.
8. Lipner cites Phillips, op. cit., p. 218: 'The difference between a man who does and a man who does not believe in God is like the difference between a man who does and a man who does not believe in a picture.'
9. J. J. Lipner, 'Does Copernicus help? Reflections for a Christian Theology of Religions', *Religious Studies*, Vol. 13, 1977, p. 258.
10. P. Tillich, *Dynamics of Faith*, Allen and Unwin, London 1957, p. 52.
11. E. Schillebeeckx, *Christ*, SCM Press, London 1980, p. 54.
12. P. Slater, 'Parables, Analogues, and Symbols', *Religious Studies* 4, October 1968, pp. 33f. This is cited by M. F. Wiles in *Faith and the Mystery of God*, SCM Press, London 1982, p. 22.
13. Wiles also makes this point before going on to apply Slater's remarks in a different connection.
14. W. C. Smith, *Towards a World Theology*, p. 189.
15. P. Tillich, *Christianity and the Encounter of the World Religions*, Columbia University Press, New York and London 1963, p. 97.

Chapter 7   Ten Years Later: Surveying the Scene

1. Wesley Ariarajah, *Hindus and Christians: a Century of Protestant Ecumenical Thought*, Eerdmans, Grand Rapids 1991, has well analysed how this tension has haunted the protestant ecumenical discussion of

religious plurality ever since the Edinburgh World Missionary Conference of 1910. Ninian Smart and Steven Konstantine, *Christian Systematic Theology in a World Context*, Marshall Pickering, Harper Collins, London 1991, embraces the new context wholeheartedly, and boldly claims to be 'the first comprehensive attempt to place the Christian faith in its real new context: that is, in the milieu of the plural and postcolonial world, and intellectually in the light of the modern study of religions (p. 17).' David J. Krieger, *The New Universalism: Foundations for a Global Theology*, Orbis Books, Maryknoll 1991, goes further: 'What is at stake in the methodological foundations of a theology of religions is nothing less than a fundamental reordering of the structure of the Western "episteme"' (p. 81).

2. Though they might not all agree with my interpretation of them, e.g.s. include: Michael Barnes, *Religions in Conversation*, SPCK, London 1989; Arnulf Camps, *Partners in Dialogue*, Orbis Books, Maryknoll 1983; Kenneth Cracknell, *Towards a New Relationship*, Epworth, London 1986; Kenneth Cragg, *The Christ and the Faiths*, SPCK, London 1986; Gavin D'Costa, *Theology and Religious Pluralism*, Blackwell, Oxford 1986; Jacques Dupuis, *Jesus Christ at the Encounter of World Religions*, Orbis Books, Maryknoll 1991; Eugene Hillman, *Many Paths*, Orbis Books, Maryknoll 1989; Hans Küng, *Global Responsibility*, SCM Press, London 1990; and *Christianity and the World Religions*, 2nd ed., SCM Press, London 1993; M.M. Thomas, *Risking Christ for Christ's Sake*, WCC, Geneva 1987.

3. Paul Knitter's classic study, *No Other Name?*, SCM Press, London/Orbis Books, Maryknoll 1985, follows similar concerns and con-clusions (with some minor disagreements) to me, but in much fuller outline and with a slightly different typology. Glyn Richards, *Towards a Theology of Religions*, Routledge, London 1989, nuances the spectrum of Christian responses very differently: Neo-Orthodox, Relativism and Inclusivism, Essentialist, Catholic, Dynamic-Typological, Dialogical, and Christocentric.

4. *The Dialogical Imperative*, p. 30.

5. Ibid., ch. 6.

6. 'Toward a Christocentric Catholic Theology', in Leonard Swidler (ed.), *Toward a Universal Theology of Religion*, Orbis Books, Maryknoll 1987, p. 91. Also: John B. Cobb, *Beyond Dialogue: Towards a Mutual Transformation of Christianity and Buddhism*, Fortress Press, Philadelphia 1982.

7. John Cobb, *Christ in a Pluralistic Age*, Westminster, Philadelphia 1975, pp. 138–39. For these reasons, I was probably over hasty to include John Cobb under 'Pluralism' in the original edition of this book. Similarly, I depicted Paul Tillich as approaching 'Pluralism' with his dynamic-typological approach (see pp. 94–97). But I now see that his commitment to the Christ, as the criterially decisive moment in history when the history of religions has manifested a concrete symbol of grace, brings him nearer to the (open) inclusivist mentality. As with Cobb,

Tillich's commitment to the decisiveness of Jesus in his earlier books survives in his last lecture, all be it in less dogmatic form.

8. Alasdair MacIntyre, *After Virtue, Whose Justice? Whose Rationality?*, Duckworth, London/University of Notre Dame Press 1988.

9. *The Gospel in a Pluralistic Society*, SPCK, London 1989, p. 166.

10. Lesslie Newbigin, 'The Gospel and Our Culture: A Response to Elaine Graham and Heather Walton', *MC*, Vol. XXXIV, No. 2, 1992, p. 9. Italics mine.

11. *Theology and Religious Pluralism*, Blackwell, Oxford 1986, p. 111.

12. *Christian Theology and Inter-religious Dialogue*, SCM Press, London 1992, p. 59. Cf. Paul Knitter, *No Other Name?*, p. 116: 'It does not seem possible to maintain this traditional insistence on the ontological necessity of Christ for salvation and at the same time coherently profess belief in the universal salvific will of the Christian God.'

13. Gavin D'Costa, 'Karl Rahner's Anonymous Christianity: A Reappraisal', *Modern Theology*, Vol. 1, No. 2, pp. 131ff., January 1985; and *Theology and Religious Pluralism*, chs 4 and 5.

14. The Baar Statement, together with conference papers and responses, are printed in *Current Dialogue*, 19, January 1991, World Council of Churches. Citations relating to this conference are taken from the relevant papers in this journal.

15. *Religions in Conversation*, SPCK, London 1989, p. 152.

16. 'The Significance of the Historical Existence of Jesus for Faith' (1911), in R. Morgan and M. Pye (eds), *Ernst Troeltsch: Writings on Theology and Religion*, Duckworth, London 1977, p. 189. I am grateful to Sarah Coakley, *Christ Without Absolutes*, OUP, Oxford 1989, p. 132 for this citation.

17. *One Christ – Many Religions*, Orbis Books, Maryknoll 1991, p. 83. Cf. John Hick, *An Interpretation of Religion*, Macmillan, London 1989, p. 246: 'When we speak of a personal God, with moral attributes and purposes, or when we speak of the non-personal Absolute, Brahman, or of the Dharmakaya, we are speaking of the Real as *humanly experienced*: that is, as phenomenon.' My italics.

18. Especially: *Problems of Religious Pluralism*, Macmillan, London 1985; *An Interpretation of Religion*, Macmillan, London 1989; and *Disputed Questions in Theology and the Philosophy of Religion*, Macmillan, London 1993.

19. John B. Cobb, 'Toward a Christocentric Catholic Theology', in Leonard Swidler (ed.), *Toward a Universal Theology of Religion*, Orbis Books, Maryknoll 1987, p. 97. Also: 'Dialogue', in *Death or Dialogue?*, ed. J. B. Cobb, M. K. Hellwig, P. F. Knitter, L. Swidler, SCM Press, London 1990.

20. Raimundo Panikkar, 'A Universal Theory or a Cosmic Confidence?', in Leonard Swidler, op. cit., p. 145. Italics mine.

21. *An Interpretation of Religion*, p. 249.

22. 'Christ, the Trinity and Religious Plurality', in *Christian Uniqueness Reconsidered*, p. 17. Other writers in this book share similar objec-

tions. See also: John Hick, 'Straightening the Record: Some Responses to Critics', *Modern Theology*, Volume 6, No. 2, January 1990, Blackwell, pp. 187–195.

23. It is incorrect of Paul Knitter in *No Other Name?*, p. 255, note 33, to suggest that I capitulate to the 'wretched historicism' warned of by Troeltsch. He forgot to read the whole of my p. 136!

24. 'Christ and the Scandal of Particularities', in *Many Mansions*, Bellew Press, London 1982.

25. *Global Responsibility*, SCM Press, London/Crossroad, New York 1991, p. 99. Cf. my 'Christianity and Other Religions: Is Inclusivism Enough?', *Theology*, Vol. LXXXIX, May 1986, No. 729, pp. 178–186, where I argue that Küng's retention of the normativity of Christ goes against the grain of his whole historical approach.

26. *A Global Ethic: The Declaration of the Parliament of the World's Religions*, ed. Hans Küng and Karl-Josef Kuschel, SCM Press, London/ Continuum, New York 1993.

27. *A Vision to Pursue*, SCM Press, London 1991, p. 190.

28. *An Interpretation of Religion*, chs 19 and 20. Also: 'The Buddha's Doctrine of the "Undetermined Questions"', and 'Religion as Skilful Means', in *Disputed Questions*, op. cit.

29. 'The Buddha and the Christ: Mediators of Liberation', R. S. Sugirtharajah, ed., *Asian Faces of Jesus*, SCM Press, London/Orbis Books, Maryknoll 1993, p. 47. Cf. John B. Cobb and Christopher Ives (eds.), *The Emptying God: a Buddhist–Jewish–Christian Conversation*, Orbis Books, Maryknoll 1990.

30. Tony Bayfield and Marcus Braybrooke (eds), *Dialogue with a Difference*, SCM Press, London 1992, ch. 1.

31. See my 'Precarious and Necessary Prophetic Witness', *Dialogue with a Difference*, op. cit., ch. 12.

INDEX OF SUBJECTS

Acts of the Apostles, 39, 42, 51,
  58f., 68
    4.12   10
    10.35   39
    14.16   39
    17.22f.   39
Areopagus speech, 39, 42, 47
Anonymous Christianity, 43,
  46–62, 68, 170
Avatara, 134
Bahai, 73
Biblical realism, 21f., 30
Brahman, 160
British Council of Churches, 5,
  169
Buddhism, 2, 43, 50, 60f., 76, 82f.,
  85, 98, 164, 166
Chinese philosophy, 93
Christ of faith, 125
Christian theology of religions
  future of, 8, 28f., 36f., 41f., 68f.,
  90, 104
  typology, 6f., 139, 149f., 151f.
Christocentrism, 152, 160
Church, 4, 8, 25, 44f., 50f., 71, 91
Church Missionary Society, 3
Common essence, 161
Common experience, 160
Comparative religion, 2, 4f., 22,
  58, 67f., 91, 112, 134f.
Conflicting truth-claims, 7, 22, 61,
  67, 73, 87ff., 94, 100f., 140,
  143ff., 164
Copernican Revolution, 82–89
Council of Chalcedon, 106, 117
Critical catalyst, 92
Dialectical theology, 14–22, 38, 93
Dialogue, 4f., 8, 11, 26f., 60, 62ff.,
  66, 68, 76, 87f., 90ff., 105,
  135ff., 144, 147, 152, 157,
  162, 163, 166, 174
Discontinuity, 22f., 35f.

Ecclesiology, 13, 15, 31f., 48–56,
  63
Ecumenism between religions, 60,
  76, 87f., 90ff., 104
Edinburgh International
  Missionary Conference, 11
Enlightenment, 24, 34, 36, 71,
  100, 123, 138, 153, 154, 165
Epistemology, 13, 19, 27ff., 36, 77,
  85f., 147, 165
Epistle to the Hebrews, 128
Eschatology, 87, 133
Essence of religion, 74f.
Evolution, 155f.
Extra-ordinary way of salvation,
  50f., 62
Finality, 10, 32, 89, 133ff., 149,
  155, 176
Fourth Gospel, 109, 125
    14.6   10
Fulfilment theory, 44, 52, 55, 57f.,
  75
General Revelation, 17ff., 22
General sacred history, 51f.
Global ethic, 164
Gospel and Our Culture, 153
Great Commission text, 15
Hinduism, 2, 16, 26, 47ff., 57–62,
  65, 82–86, 93, 97, 143
Historical consciousness, 1f., 6ff.
  28–37, 41f., 53, 56ff., 62,
  68ff., 78f., 104, 123f., 136,
  138, 140ff., 159
Historical criticism, 30ff., 108f.,
  112, 123f., 154, 159
Historicism, 78ff.
History of religions, 2, 4f., 14, 21,
  29, 41, 55, 58, 69, 78f., 82,
  94ff., 98ff., 104
Holy Spirit, 157
Ideology, 4f., 11, 26, 40, 99
Indifference, 73

Index of Subjects

Islam, 8, 21, 50, 60f., 76, 82, 93

Jerusalem International Missionary Conference, 11

Jesus of history, 40f., 58, 66, 109, 125, 130f., 136

Judaism, 1, 21, 36, 40, 42, 83, 133, 149, 156

Kenotic christology, 116, 120

Krishna, 65, 135

Layman's Missionary Movement of N. America, 72

Liberal theology, 14, 21, 29, 71ff.

Liberation, 159, 166

Logos theology, 42f., 55, 59, 71, 98, 152

Luke's Gospel, 36, 39ff., 51f., 55,

  4.21   40

  24.27   40

  3.38   41

Mazdaism, 21

Mission, 2, 8, 11, 13, 15, 21, 23f., 48ff., 72, 153

Mysticism, 21, 64ff., 83, 85, 88, 94ff., 167

Myth, 65f., 89f., 93, 117–124, 133f., 145

Natural theology, 19, 22

Neo-orthodoxy, 22

Noumenal world, 86

Ordinary way of salvation, 50f., 62

Orthodox Church, 39, 50f.

Outside the Church no salvation, 10, 25, 45, 49.

Paedagogos, 43f.

Paradox, 88, 109f., 114f.

Particularity, 86f., 144, 147f.

Paul, 36, 40, 55, 174

Phenomenal world, 86

Phenomenology of religious experience, 84f., 96f., 150

Plurality of ultimates, 161

Points of contact, 38, 59, 61, 88

Praeparatio evangelica, 43f., 59

Pre-existence, 117, 119ff., 126ff.

Process theology, 66, 128ff., 151

Prophetic religion, 21, 64ff., 83, 85, 94ff.

Reconception, 74ff., 172

Relativism, 8, 20, 29, 31, 60, 63f., 66, 69, 76–80, 90, 95–100, 104, 135, 142, 172

Salvation history, 43, 46f., 50ff., 79, 164

Sat-cit-ananda, 160

Scandal of particularity 108f.

Second Vatican Council, 4, 39, 43ff., 53–58, 67f., 71f., 110, 135, 170

Sola fide, 35, 37

Sovereignty of God, 12ff., 17, 19, 22, 27ff., 155, 162, 167

Special sacred history, 51f.

Story, 118f.

Stromata, 43

Supernatural existential, 46, 56

Syncretism, 73, 76, 78, 104 136

Tambaram International Missionary Conference, 11, 21

Tolerance, 71f., 76

Trinity, 157f., 161

Truth

  Christianity as final arbiter of, 11, 13ff., 26, 29, 37, 45, 64ff., 108, 134, 153, 163

  common search for, 63–67, 72, 92f., 104, 136, 144

  creative tension, 54, 63–66, 88, 136, 147f., 166

  diverse expression, 20, 44, 60, 64, 67, 72ff., 76, 81, 83, 87, 92, 101, 104, 144

  eschatalogical verification, 87, 146f.

  ethical criteria, 159, 163

  God as final arbiter of, 60f., 83ff., 90, 146f.

  humane, 100, 102

  prejudging, 62f., 67ff., 75, 103, 112, 135, 155, 157

  truth for us, 80

Vedanta, 61, 86, 171

World Council of Churches, 4, 11, 22, 50, 91, 156, 174

World's Parliament of Religions, 163

INDEX OF NAMES

Abe, Masao, 98
Abhishiktananda, 59,171
Anderson, G. H., 168
Aquinas, 61
Ariarajah, W., 177
Augustine, 48, 106
Baillie, D. M., 114f., 175
Barnes, M., 157, 178
Barth, Karl, 11-30, 33, 35f., 45,
    49f., 70, 72, 78, 95, 108ff.,
    141, 151, 152, 168, 175
Bartsch, H. W., 175
Bayfield, Tony, 166, 180
Berger, P. T., 141ff., 177
Bleeker, C. J., 168
Boniface VIII (Pope), 10
Bowden, J., 109, 175
Braybrooke, M., 180
Brunner, E., 11, 17–21. 25f., 37f.,
    169
Bultmann, R., 117f., 141
Camps, A., 178
Carmen, J., 168
Chakkarai, V., 128
Clayton, J. P., 176
Clement of Alexandria, 43
Cobb, J. B., 98f., 152, 160, 161,
    173f., 178, 179, 180
Cracknell, K., 4, 178
Cragg, A. K., 30, 169, 172, 178
Dawe, D., 168
D'Costa, G., 155f., 158, 162, 178,
    179
Dewick, E. C., 171
Dionysius, 61
Drury, J., 55, 169, 171
Dupuis, J., 54, 171, 178
Dyson, A. O., 79, 93, 173f.
Eckhart, Meister, 85
Eliade, M., 4
Farquhar, J. N., 57f., 68
Feuerbach, 173

Flannery, A., 175
Ford, D. F., 27, 169
Forrester, D. B., 86, 173
Gispert-Sauch, G., 170
Goulder, M., 116, 169, 175
Griffiths, B., 59ff., 171
Hallencreutz, C. F., 7
Harnack, A. V., 124
Hebblethwaite, B. L., 106, 111
    116, 121f., 172f., 175f.
Hegel, G. W. F., 18, 73
Hellwig, M., 179
Hick, J. H., 71, 82–90, 94, 96, 103,
    133f., 143, 158, 160, 161, 164,
    172–75, 177, 179, 180
Hillman, E., 49, 51, 170, 178
Hocking, W. E., 71, 74ff., 172
Hooft, W. A. Visser't, 11, 22
Houlden, J. L., 125f., 128, 176
Jaspers, K., 82
Kant, 18, 85f.
Khodr, G., 50, 170
Kierkegaard, S., 142
Klostermaier, K., 59
Knitter, P., 157, 158, 178, 179,
    180
Knox, J., 120ff., 128, 176
Konstantine, S., 178
Kraemer, H., 11, 16–26, 30ff.,
    37f., 70, 72, 78, 168f.
Krieger, D., 178
Küng, H., 25, 41f., 45, 49f.,
    62–69, 92f., 122, 163, 168f.,
    171, 178, 180
Kuschel, K.-J., 180
Lampe, G. W. H., 119, 176
Lessing, 78, 173
Lipner, J. J., 144ff., 173, 177
Lochhead, D., 151
de Lubac, H., 53, 55
MacIntyre, A., 153, 179
Martyr, Justin, 42ff., 59

Index of Names

Merton, T., 60, 171
Moltmann, J., 176
Moule, C. F. D., 125ff., 176
Neuner, J., 168f.
Newbigin, L., 11, 25, 34ff., 136, 152ff., 169, 173, 179
Nicholas of Cusa, 71
Niles, D. T., 16
Nineham, D. E., 176
Otto, R., 18
Panikkar, R., 47, 59, 161, 170, 179
Pathrapankal, J., 171
Phillips, D. Z., 145, 147
Pieris, A., 166
Pittenger, N., 109, 130, 133ff., 175ff.
Pius IX (Pope), 25
Powell, B., 117
Rahner, Karl, 43, 45–68, 71, 110, 112, 155f., 170, 175
Richards, G., 178
Richmond, J., 175
Robinson, J. A. T., 63–68, 88, 96, 120ff., 133ff., 171, 176f.
Rogers, C. M., 174
Röper, A., 56
Samartha, S., 160, 174
Sankara, 61
Schillebeeckx, E., 124, 130ff., 146, 176f.
Schleiermacher, F., 18, 141f.

Schlette, H. R., 51, 53, 170
Sharpe, E. J., 7, 58, 91, 168, 171, 174
Slater, P., 147, 177
Smart, N., 85, 173, 178
Smith, D. H., 90, 174
Smith, W. C., 2, 25, 70f., 99–103, 144, 147, 168
Strauss, D. F., 117
Sugirtharajah, R. S., 180
Swidler, L., 178, 179
Sykes, S. W., 169, 176
Taylor, J. V., 175
Temple, W., 21
Thomas, M. M., 178
Thomas, O. C., 7, 172f.
Tillich, P., 3f., 71, 85, 94ff., 143, 146, 148, 168, 172, 174, 177, 179
Toynbee, A., 71ff., 76, 172
Troeltsch, E., 29, 71, 78ff., 90, 95f., 173
Tyrell, G., 124
Veitch, J. A., 5, 16, 168
Vidler, A. R., 173
Ward, K., 121f., 129, 164, 176
Warren, M., 3
Wiles, M. F., 56, 76, 120ff., 155, 171f., 175, 177
Young, F., 136, 177
Zaehner, R. C., 97, 174